# LISTEN!
# AND HELP TELL THE STORY

# LISTEN!
# AND HELP TELL THE STORY

By Bernice Wells Carlson

*illustrations by Burmah Burris*

ABINGDON PRESS

NASHVILLE      NEW YORK

*The Story ONE EGG? TWO EGGS? by Yoshiko Yokochi is included in this collection with the permission of the author.*

Copyright © 1965 by Abingdon Press. All Rights Reserved. Lithographed in the United States of America. Library of Congress Catalog Number: 65-14090. ISBN 0-687-22096-3.

*To my grandson*
*David Carlson Umberger*

I should like to thank the many boys and girls who helped me prepare this book: neighborhood children, children in public-school classes, a private nursery school and a church recreation group. I should like to thank also a number of people who offered professional advice, especially two teachers: David Ginglend of Lincoln School, Plainfield, New Jersey, and Mrs. Edmond Samuel of Antioch School, Prekindergarten Group, Yellow Springs, Ohio. Mrs. Samuel is the former Yoshiko Yokochi, a native of Nagoya, Japan.

# CONTENTS

## INTRODUCTION

"We learn to listen in order to listen to learn." The old adage is as true today as when it first was uttered. It is true for every field of learning and for every age group.

A child's listening training cannot start too early and it must be a continuous process. As he learns to listen to increasingly difficult material he learns also to remember, to think, and to respond. Learning to listen should be a natural process, not a matter of forced drill. A child or an adult should listen because he wants to do so.

How can you teach a child to listen? How can you prompt him to *want* to listen? There is no simple answer. Any activity that encourages him to listen for fun should be explored and used.

In each activity in this book a child is asked to help tell a story by responding to a cue with either an action, a single sound, a phrase, or a chorus. He cannot make the proper response unless he first listens.

This collection contains a variety of stories and story poems, all chosen because children have liked the sound of the words or noises, the tempo of the verse or story, and the subject matter. They challenge a child's imagination, appeal to his interests and experiences, and offer a variety of activities.

The range is wide. Included are old nursery rhymes and favorite poems, used here for a special purpose; new stories and poems written especially for this book; ballads and tales from the realm of fantasy; material based on everyday reality such as home, weather, and familiar noises; rollicking nonsense; beautiful poetry; and stories that quicken the senses and provoke thought.

This book may be used with an individual child or with a group of children, ranging in age from preschool through the early grades. The activities are fun to do at home or in class. Some activities are suitable for group meetings, such as Brownie Scouts or Cub Scouts. Some of the poems are suitable for programs. In general the book progresses from verses for the preschool child to slightly more difficult material. Within each chapter, the simplest material comes first. At the end of each selection the child or group is quiet, ready to listen to the next thing the speaker has to say.

This is a child's own book. Chapter introductions and directions are addressed to the adult reader, or storyteller, but the stories and story poems are for the child. Let him turn the pages and look at the pictures. Before you read or recite one of the verses, get the child's undivided attention. If he is a very young child, or a child with a short attention span, remove from his reach any objects that might distract him. Tell him about the verse or story and explain what he is expected to do. Read in a rhythmic manner. Choose selections from one part of the book and then another, or let the child choose.

Encourage the child to join you in making the expected response, in making the action or in saying the sound or phrase, but if he fails to do so do not scold him or retard the flow of the story.

Praise the child or the group who listens. Without preaching you will demonstrate that it is fun to listen.

# FINGER PLAYS
## OR HANDIES

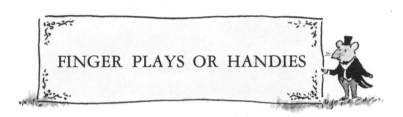

# FINGER PLAYS OR HANDIES

Hands and arms help tell the story. Very often a child will pay attention to the movement of your fingers and arms before he will pay attention to what you are saying. He will copy your actions before he will repeat your words. When he becomes interested in finger plays, or handies, he is consciously or unconsciously making an association between speech and motion. He cannot make this association unless he listens.

Finger play is fun. It gives a child and an adult an opportunity to communicate before a child is ready to carry on a conversation.

Finger play can be an introduction to story time. In the verses given here something always happens. Not much, but something. When something happens there is a little story. When a child listens to the verse, he is listening to the little story. When he moves his fingers, his hands, or his arms as directed, he is helping to tell the story by acting it out.

Finger play can help a child to develop in other ways. His ears pick up the rhyme of the verse, a help in learning to distinguish and identify sounds and a very valuable aid in speech development.

Many finger-play activities help develop the meaning of abstract concepts as hands go "up and down," "in and out," and "open and shut."

When doing finger play a child uses small muscles of his hands which might otherwise be neglected. He develops a sense of rhythm, for all nursery rhymes have a definite beat, and a sense of rhythm aids body coordination.

It is better to recite a finger-play activity than to read it. Without the book you can pay full attention to the child and he will pay full attention to what you are saying and doing. Say the verse slowly and distinctly; the younger the child, the slower your speech should be. Accent the rhythm of the verse.

Don't force the child to make the motions you are making or to say the words you are saying. Remain flexible, enjoying any reaction you may get. The average five-year-old who is interested in a verse will copy your actions at once and soon repeat the words of the verse. The reactions of a younger child will vary. He may want you to repeat a finger-play verse using your hands. He may imitate you part of the time. He may want to count on *your* fingers, or he may want you to count on his fingers. He may join you in saying one phrase or one line. He may not appear to respond at all. If a young child does not respond at first, don't be discouraged. There may be some reason for his hesitation. He may be building up an "inner vocabulary" by trying to understand the meaning of the words before he uses them. He may need to bolster his self-confidence before he tries to imitate your actions or your speech. He may want to make sure he understands what you want him to do before he responds.

If he seems to like the lilt of your voice, the rhythm of your speech, or the motions of your hands, he is listening. If he wants to hear the verse or story a second, third, or fourth time, he is listening.

Praise him when he cooperates in any way. The chances are that eventually he will respond as he is expected to do.

## JACK-IN-THE-BOX

This is Jack    (*Clench left fist with thumb extended*)

In a box.    (*Put thumb in fist. Cover with palm of right hand*)

Open the lid,    (*Lift right hand*)

Out Jack pops!    (*Pull thumb out of fist with a jerk*)

—BERNICE WELLS CARLSON
(*Party Book for Boys and Girls*)

## THE BEEHIVE

Here is the beehive.          (*Hold up clenched fist*)
Where are the bees?
Hiding away where nobody
    sees?
Look! They are coming out!    (*Loosen fist slightly*)
They are all alive!
One! Two! Three! Four! Five!   (*Lift one finger at a time*)

—EMILIE POULSSON (*Finger Play for Nursery and Kindergarten*)

## HICKORY, DICKORY DOCK

Hickory, dickory dock!  (*Swing arms back and forth as a pendulum swings*)

The mouse ran up the clock.  (*Put hands close together for one mouse. Wiggle fingers as you raise arms above head*)

The clock struck one!  (*Clap hands above head*)

The mouse ran down.  (*Put hands close together. Wiggle fingers as you lower arms*)

Hickory, dickory dock!  (*Swing arms as a pendulum*)

—MOTHER GOOSE

# TWO COZY HOMES

| | |
|---|---|
| Two cozy homes | |
| Stand upon a hill. | (*Put fists on table*) |
| Here lives Jack. | (*Lift and then lower left fist*) |
| Here lives Jill. | (*Lift and then lower right fist*) |
| | |
| When they've had breakfast | |
| They go out to play. | (*Extend two forefingers*) |
| They run | (*Move extended fingers rapidly*) |
| And they jump | (*Lift and lower arms*) |
| And they swing all day. | (*Swing arms back and forth*) |
| When the sun goes down | |
| They go in to stay. | |
| Here rests Jack. | (*Rest fists on table*) |
| Here rests Jill. | (*Lift and lower left fist*) |
| Everything is quiet | (*Lift and lower right fist*) |
| Upon the little hill. | (*Fold hands on table*) |

—BERNICE WELLS CARLSON

## JOHNNY'S RIDE

Johnny looked at the moon.　　*(Stretch arms over head. Hold hands in the shape of a moon)*

Johnny looked at the stars.　　*(With arms still lifted, wiggle fingers for twinkling stars)*

Johnny got in a rocket.　　*(Lower arms to waist. Place palms and fingers together in shape of a rocket cone)*

Johnny went up to Mars.　　*(With hands still together, lift arms quickly as high as you can over your head)*

—ADAPTED BY BERNICE WELLS CARLSON

## THIS LITTLE COW

*(Point to each finger as you say verse. On word "lay" in last line drop hands, palms down, on lap)*

This little cow ate grass.
This little cow ate hay.
This little cow drank water.
This little cow ran away.
This little cow did nothing.
She just lay down all day.

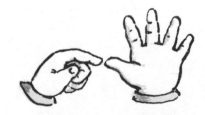

—ADAPTED FROM MOTHER GOOSE

## FIVE ROYAL PENGUINS

*(Clench left fist with the thumb extended. As you mention each num-ber, raise another finger. At the end of the verses count the raised fingers, starting with the little finger and pointing to each one with the index finger of the other hand. After "four" swoop down the side of the index finger and up the thumb, saying "F-i-v-e" slowly)*

One royal penguin,
Nothing much to do,
Called for his brother,
Then there were two.

Two royal penguins,
Happy as could be,
Called for their sister,
Then there were three.

Three royal penguins,
Wished there were more,
Called for their mother,
Then there were four.

Four royal penguins,
Learning how to dive,
Called for their father,
Then there were five.

One, two, three, four, f-i-v-e!

—BERNICE WELLS CARLSON

## FIVE BIRTHDAY CANDLES

*(Raise one hand with fingers extended. Starting with thumb, lower one finger each time you blow out a candle)*

Five birthday candles;
Wish there were more.
Blow out one                    *(Blow quickly)*
Then there are four.

Four birthday candles
Pretty as can be.
Blow out one                    *(Blow quickly)*
Then there are three.

Three birthday candles;
Mother bought them new.
Blow out one                    *(Blow quickly)*
Then there are two.

Two birthday candles—
Birthday cakes are fun.
Blow out one                    *(Blow quickly)*
Then there is one.

One birthday candle—
A birthday wish is fun.        *(Pause)*
Blow out one                    *(Blow slowly)*
Then there is none.

—BERNICE WELLS CARLSON

# THE FIVE BLACK CATS AND THE WITCH

*(Hold up five fingers of left hand. Lower one finger as you say each vowel sound. Speak slowly, drawing out the sound of the vowel. For the second verse, hold up the right fist, clenched. Raise one finger as you say each vowel sound. Speak quickly. Clap at end)*

Five black cats sat on a fence,
Waiting for Hallowe'en.
    *(Raise five fingers of left hand, palm facing out)*
One said, "Say!"
    *(Lower thumb)*
One said, "See!"
    *(Lower index finger)*
One said, "Sigh!"
    *(Lower middle finger)*
One said, "So!"
    *(Lower ring finger)*
One said, "Soo-oo-oo!"
    *(Lower little finger so fist is closed)*

The old witch came and shouted,
While looking rather mean:
    *(Raise clenched fist of right hand)*
"A!"
    *(Raise thumb)*
"E!"
    *(Raise index finger)*
"I!"
    *(Raise middle finger)*
"O!"
    *(Raise ring finger)*
"U!"
    *(Raise little finger)*
"Scadoo-o-o!"
    *(Clap hands)*

—ADAPTED BY BERNICE WELLS CARLSON

## THE LITTLE FISH

*(Put your left hand out, palm down, fingers closed, and thumb sticking out. Put your right hand on top of your left, palm also down and thumb sticking out. This is a fish with fins at its sides. Wiggle the thumbs. Make the fish swim by moving hands up and down in unison. Then make fish swim and wiggle fins at the same time. Open the mouth. Keep palms together, but drop the lefthand fingers and raise the right-hand fingers. Close the mouth on "takes a bite.")*

Little fish                          *(Place palms in above position)*
Goes out to play.

He wiggles his fins,                 *(Wiggle thumbs)*
Then swims away.                     *(Move fingers up and down in unison)*


He swims and swims                   *(Move fingers up and down in unison and wiggle thumbs)*
In the water bright.
He opens his mouth                   *(Keep palms together, lower fingers of left hand, raise fingers of right hand)*

And takes a bite.                    *(Close to starting position)*
Mmmmmmmmmm!  Tastes
  good!

—BERNICE WELLS CARLSON (FROM PLAY ACTIVITIES FOR THE RETARDED CHILD *by Bernice Wells Carlson and David R. Ginglend*)

## TWO CATS OF KILKENNY

There once were two cats of
  Kilkenny.
Each thought there was one
  cat too many.
So they fought and they fit.
They scratched and they bit.
'Til except for their nails
And the tips of their tails,
Instead of two cats
There weren't any!

(*Hold up clenched fists to represent cats*)

(*Rub fists together as two cats fighting*)
(*Open hands very slowly with palms outstretched*)
(*Look at empty palms. Shake head*)

—MOTHER GOOSE

## THE TOAD'S SONG

*(In this poem the right fist is the little toad which jumps about. Lay your fist flat on a table or in your lap. Curl your left hand around it, to make a little cell under the stone)*

| | |
|---|---|
| I am a little toad | *(Right fist rests quietly, sheltered* |
| Living by the road. | *by left hand)* |
| Beneath a stone I dwell | |
| Snug in a little cell. | |
| Hip, hip, hop. | *(Move right fist up and down,* |
| Hip, hip, hop! | *behind left hand)* |
| | |
| Just listen to my song. | *(Right hand is still)* |
| I sleep all winter long | |
| But in the spring I peep out | *(Move right fist from behind left* |
| And then I jump about. | *hand, and have it jump* |
| Hip, hip, hop. | *about)* |
| Hip, hip, hop! | |
| | |
| And now I catch a fly | *(Make grabbing motion with* |
| Before he winks an eye. | *right hand)* |
| And now I take a hop | *(Making hopping motion until* |
| And now and then I stop. | *word "stop")* |
| Hip, hip, hop. | |
| Hip, hip, hop! Stop! | |

—BASED ON OLD ENGLISH NURSERY RHYME

30

## ONCE I CAUGHT A FISH ALIVE

One, two, three, four, five!     (*Point to fingers as you count*)
Once I caught a fish alive.
Six, seven, eight, nine, ten!     (*Point to fingers as you count*)
Then I let it go again.     (*Make motion of throwing fish
                in brook*)


Why did I let it go?
Because it bit my finger so.
Which finger did it bite?
The little finger on the right.     (*Point to little finger on right
                hand*)

—MOTHER GOOSE

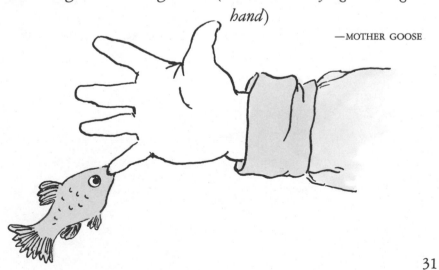

## TEN SILLY SPACEMEN

*(Hold up ten fingers; lower one each time a spaceman goes away)*

Ten silly spacemen
In a cafeteria line.
One got out of place
Then there were nine.

Nine silly spacemen
Learning how to skate.
One went on thin ice
Then there were eight.

Eight silly spacemen
Looking up at heaven.
One tumbled backward
Then there were seven.

Seven silly spacemen
Doing fancy tricks.
One jumped off a roof
Then there were six.

Six silly spacemen
Watching a beehive.
One stuck in his nose
Then there were five.

Five silly spacemen
Eating more and more.
One ate thirty cakes
Then there were four.

Four silly spacemen
Climbing up a tree.
One swung from a twig
Then there were three.

Three silly spacemen
Can't find much to do.
One fell fast asleep
Then there were two.

Two silly spacemen
Looking for some fun.
One caught a kite's tail
Then there was one.

One silly spaceman—
Now our story's done;
He rode a rocket,
Then there was none.

—BERNICE WELLS CARLSON

10 9 8 7 6 5 4 3 2 1

## MAKE THE PLUM PUDDING

| | |
|---|---|
| Into a big bowl put the plums | (*Put plums in bowl*) |
| Stir-about, stir-about, stir-about, stir! | (*Stir*) |
| Next the good white flour comes; | (*Add flour*) |
| Stir-about, stir-about, stir-about, stir! | (*Stir*) |
| Add sugar, and peel, eggs, and spice; | (*Add new ingredients*) |
| Stir-about, stir-about, stir-about, stir! | (*Stir*) |
| Mix them and fix them | (*Stir again and taste*) |
| And cook them twice. | (*Place bowl in oven*) |
| Then eat it up! Eat it up! Eat it up! | (*Eat*) |
| UMMMMMMMM! | (*Rub stomach*) |

—BASED ON OLD ENGLISH RHYME

33

## TEN FINGERS

*(Move fingers as action is described in verses)*

I have ten little fingers
With which I like to play.
They can be such different
    things
On any kind of day.

*(Hold up hands with fingers spread apart)*

Now they're ten ants running
In the summer sun.
Hither, thither darting,
Work is never done.

*(Move fingers lightly across table or lap)*

Now they're ten fish swim-
    ming
In a gurgling brook.
Safe from larger fishes,
Safe from any hook.

*(Put palms together. Wiggle hands back and forth at wrist in swimming motion)*

| Now they're spiders climbing | (*Wiggle fingers as you raise* |
| Up a silken line, | *arms*) |
| Safe in corners hiding | |
| From your eyes and mine. | |

| Now they are ten fingers | (*Hold up hands with fingers* |
| In a row like this. | *spread apart*) |
| They can help me clap my | (*Clap hands*) |
| hands | |
| And throw you a big kiss. | (*Throw kiss*) |

(*Say the next lines as quickly as you can*)

| Ants running, | (*Move fingers rapidly on table* |
| | *or lap*) |
| Fish swimming, | (*Make swimming motion with* |
| | *hands*) |
| Spiders climbing, | (*Wiggle fingers as you raise* |
| | *arms*) |
| Hands clapping. | (*Give two short claps*) |

| Bang! | (*Give one big clap*) |

—TRADITIONAL VERSE ADAPTED BY BERNICE WELLS CARLSON

## THE PUPPY AND THE KITTY CAT

| | |
|---|---|
| Here is a little puppy. | (*Hold up left fist*) |
| Here is a kitty cat. | (*Hold up right fist*) |
| | |
| Puppy goes to sleep, | (*Put clenched fist, fingers down,* |
| Curled up on his mat. | *on table or lap*) |
| | |
| Kitty creeps up softly, | (*Move fingers of right hand* |
| | *slowly toward left hand.* |
| Tickles puppy's chin. | *Tickle thumb of left hand* |
| | *with index finger of right*) |
| | |
| Puppy wakes up quickly! | (*Lift left fist*) |
| See the chase begin! | (*Keeping fingers clenched, have* |
| | *left hand "chase" right in* |
| | *circles*) |

—ADAPTED BY BERNICE WELLS CARLSON

## THE OWL AND THE BROWNIES

An owl sat alone         *(Sit quietly with hands folded*
On the branch of a tree.     *in lap)*
And he was as quiet
As quiet could be.

It was night and his eyes     *(Cup hands in half circles. Hold*
Were round, like this.       *up to eyes)*
He looked around. Not a     *(Look around)*
Thing did he miss.

Some brownies crept up     *(Make fingers of one hand creep*
On a branch of the tree,     *on back of the other hand and*
And they were as quiet      *up the arm)*
As quiet could be.

Said the wise old owl,
"To-whooo! To-whooo!"
Up jumped the brownies     *(Raise both arms)*
And away they all flew.      *(Making flying motions)*

The owl sat alone
On the branch of the tree
And he was as quiet       *(Sit quietly with hands folded*
As quiet could be.         *in lap)*

—MAUDE BURNHAM

# FIVE LITTLE CHICKENS

*(The fingers on one hand are the five little chicks. Your thumb is the first little chick. Hold it up when the first chick speaks. Hold up one more finger as each chick speaks. The fist of your other hand is the big mother hen. Move it as she speaks)*

Said the first little chicken,　　　　*(Hold up thumb)*
With a queer little squirm,
"I wish I could find
A fat little worm."

Said the second little chicken,　　　*(Hold up index finger)*
With an odd little shrug,
"I wish I could find
A fat little bug."

Said the third little chicken,　　　　*(Hold up middle finger)*
With a sharp little squeal,
"I wish I could find
Some nice yellow meal."

Said the fourth little chicken,      (*Hold up ring finger*)
With a sigh of grief,
"I wish I could find
A little green leaf."

Said the fifth little chicken,      (*Hold up little finger*)
With a faint little moan,
"I wish I could find
A wee gravel stone."

"Now, see here," said the      (*Hold up fist of opposite hand*)
      mother,
From the green garden patch,
"If you want any breakfast,
Just come here and scratch!"

—TRADITIONAL

ACTION VERSES

ACTION VERSES

These story poems are more difficult to act out than finger-play verses because there is more activity. A child must listen very carefully in order to know when to start, and when to stop, a motion. By acting out these verses he develops coordination between speech and rhythmic body motions.

In most cases the adult does the action with the child. The child watches as well as listens in order to know what to do. Sometimes the adult tells the child what to do, as "Get on my knee. We'll bounce together as I tell the story." Or the adult asks the child how he would illustrate a motion in a given line as, "Ride a pony." The child must listen in order to do the action at the right time.

You probably know most of these jingles or versions of them. Memorize them or at least be able to say them by looking only occasionally at the book. You should be free to join the child in acting out the verses.

Some children like to make up verses of their own, patterned after those given here. If a child shows such an interest by all means encourage him. If he makes up a verse be sure that *you* listen to *him!*

## LITTLE ROBIN REDBREAST

Little Robin Redbreast
Sat upon a rail.
Niddle-naddle went his head,  (*Bob head up and down*)
Wiggle-waggle went his tail.  (*Wiggle backside*)

—MOTHER GOOSE

## JEREMIAH BLEW THE FIRE

Jeremiah blew the fire;
Puff, puff, puff!  (*Blow*)
First he blew it gently;  (*Puff gently*)
Then he blew it rough.  (*Blow hard*)

—ADAPTED FROM OLD ENGLISH RHYME

45

# THIS IS THE WAY THE LADY RIDES

*(Cross your knees; hold child on your lap, clasping one of his hands in each of yours)*

| | |
|---|---|
| This is the way the lady rides;<br>Prim, prim, prim. | *(Sit very straight and bounce child slowly)* |
| This is the way the gentle-<br>man rides;<br>Trim, trim, trim. | *(Bounce a little faster)* |
| But this is the way the farmer<br>rides;<br>Bumpety, bumpety, bump! | *(Rock child back and forth on your knee)* |

*(When the child knows the above, try a slightly different version with a greater climax)*

| | |
|---|---|
| One day the lady rode to the<br>fair;<br>Prim, prim, prim. | *(Bounce child slowly on knee)* |
| The gentleman rode to meet<br>her there;<br>Trim, trim, trim. | *(Bounce faster)* |
| But when the farmer rode to<br>town,<br>His horse hit a stump<br>And he fell down;<br>Bumpety, bump! | *(Rock child back and forth on knee)*<br>*(Lower your legs quickly, letting child slide to your feet as you continue to hold his hands)* |

—TRADITIONAL RHYME

## THE FARMER
## AND THE GRAY MARE

*(Cross your knees. Hold child on your lap, clasping one of his hands in each of yours)*

A farmer went trotting
Upon his gray mare;
Bumpety, bumpety, bump!

*(Bounce child up and down on knee with heavy bump)*

With his daughter behind
him,
So healthy and fair;
Lumpety, lumpety, lump!

*(Rock child back and forth on knee)*

An owl cried "Whooo!"
They all tumbled down,
Bumpety, bumpety, bump!
The mare broke her knees,
The farmer his crown;
Lumpety, lumpety, lump!

*(Stop)*
*(Lower knees. Still holding child's hands, let him slide to floor. Rock legs back and forth.)*

— TRADITIONAL

48

## PITTER, PATTER GOES THE RAIN

Pitter, patter goes the rain.
Splash, splash go my feet.

Crash! Goes the thunder!
I run down the street.

*(Tap gently with fingertips)*
*(Stamp feet softly as if in puddles)*
*(Clap hands on "crash")*
*(Move two fingers forward quickly, as if running; or move feet up and down though staying in one place)*

—BERNICE WELLS CARLSON

## LIKE LEAVES IN WINDY WEATHER

*(Each child may twirl alone, or children may grasp hands, form a circle, and dance around together)*

Dance and twirl together            *(Dance and twirl around)*
Like leaves in windy weather.
Puff! Puff! Puff!                    *(Stand still. Blow)*
All fall down.                       *(Fall down)*

—BERNICE WELLS CARLSON

## THE RABBIT

I saw a little rabbit come      (*Make hopping motions with*
  Hop, hop, hop!               *hands and arms*)

I saw his two long ears go      (*Put hands at sides of head*)
  Flop, flop, flop!            (*Flop hands up and down*)
I saw his little nose go
  Twink, twink, twink.      (*Wiggle nose*)
I saw his little eyes go
  Wink, wink, wink.       (*Wink eyes*)
I said, "Little rabbit,
  won't you stay?"
Then he looked at me,       (*Pause and stare*)
  And hopped away.       (*Make fast hopping motions
                      with hands and arms*)

—BERNICE WELLS CARLSON

## SPACE ROCKET

*(Sit with elbows close to the body and hands held in front with tips of fingers touching to form cone of a rocket)*

Inside a rocket ship,
Just enough room.
Here comes the countdown—
10, 9, 8, 7, 6, 5, 4, 3, 2, 1, 0,
And Zoo-o-o-o-o-o-om!

*(Stand up and raise arms as high as possible with fingers still held together like the cone of a rocket)*

—BERNICE WELLS CARLSON

## MR. TALL AND MR. SMALL

| | |
|---|---|
| There once was a man | (*Stand on tiptoes. Reach up as* |
| Who was tall, tall, tall. | *far as possible*) |
| He had a friend | |
| Who was small, small, small. | (*Kneel and bend 'way down*) |
| | |
| The man who was small | (*Cup hands near mouth. Look* |
| Would try to call | *up.*) |
| To the man who was tall, | |
| "Hello, up there!" | (*In high voice*) |
| | |
| The man who was tall | (*Stand on tiptoes*) |
| At once would call | |
| To the man who was small, | (*Bend from waist*) |
| "Hello, down there." | (*Use deep voice*) |
| | |
| Then each tipped his hat | (*Stand straight*) |
| And made this reply: | (*Tip an imaginary hat*) |
| "Good-bye, my friend." | (*Look up, speak in high voice*) |
| "Good-bye, good-bye." | (*Bow, and speak in deep voice*) |

—BERNICE WELLS CARLSON

# POOR DOG! POOR MO!

*(The listener repeats each line after he hears it)*

| | |
|---|---|
| There once was a man, | *(Repeat line)* |
| His name was Mo. | *(Repeat line)* |
| He took his dog | *(Repeat line)* |
| Wherever he'd go. | *(Repeat line)* |
| | |
| They climbed to a hilltop, | *(Repeat line and reach up high)* |
| | |
| Went down on a sled, | *(Repeat line and scoop down with hands)* |
| | |
| Bumped into a tree, | *(Repeat line and put hands on head)* |
| | |
| And landed in bed. | *(Repeat line. Keep hands on head and rock back and forth)* |
| | |
| Poor Mo! Oh! Oh! | *(Repeat line)* |
| Poor dog! Bow wow! | *(Repeat line. Rock hard. Stop suddenly)* |
| Stop dog! Stop! | |
| You're crowding me now. | |

—BERNICE WELLS CARLSON

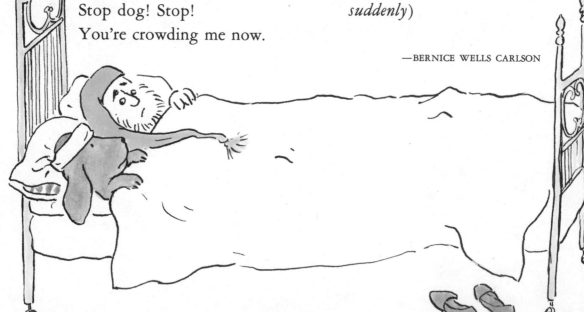

## TWO LITTLE GHOSTS

A very old witch was
Stirring a pot.
Ooo-ooo! Ooo-ooo!

*(Make stirring motion)*
*(Say this sound in two syllables:*
  $\overline{oo}$-$\overline{oo}$)

Two little ghosts said
"What has she got?"
Ooo-ooo! Ooo-ooo!

*(Put hands on hips; bend over*
  *as if looking in pot)*

Tiptoe. Tiptoe. Tip—
Boooo!

*(Make fingers creep forward)*
*(Raise hands high over head.*
  *Jump up)*

—ADAPTED BY BERNICE WELLS CARLSON

# OVER IN THE MEADOW

*(Hold up the correct number of fingers each time a number is mentioned.
Pantomime the actions)*

Over in the meadow,
In the sand, in the sun
Lived an old mother toad
And her toadie one.                          *(Hold up one finger)*
"Wink!" said the mother.                      *(Wink)*
"I wink," said the one.                       *(Wink)*
So they winked and blinked                    *(Wink and blink)*
In the sand, in the sun.

Over in the meadow,
Where the stream runs blue,
Lived an old mother fish
And her little fishes two.                    *(Hold up two fingers)*
"Swim!" said the mother.                      *(Pantomime swimming)*
"We swim," said the two.                      *(Pantomime swimming)*
So they swam and they leaped                  *(Pantomime swimming and*
Where the stream runs blue.                      *leaping with hands)*

Over in the meadow,
In a hole in the tree,
Lived a mother bluebird
And her little birdies three.     (*Hold up three fingers*)
"Sing!" said the mother.          (*Fold hands across chest. Lift chest*)

"We sing," said the three.        (*Pantomime singing*)
So they sang and were glad
In the hole in the tree.

Over in the meadow,
In the reeds on the shore,
Lived a mother muskrat
And her little muskrats four.      (*Hold up four fingers*)
"Dive," said the mother.           (*Pantomime diving*)
"We dive," said the four.          (*Pantomime diving*)
So they dived and they bur-        (*Pantomime diving and bur-
   rowed,                             rowing*)
In the reeds on the shore.

—OLIVE A. WADSWORTH

59

## LET'S PRETEND

*(Before you read a verse, ask a child how he would make the motion which the verse suggests, such as "How do you ride a pony?" Ask him how the pony would fall down. Emphasize the fact that the child must stop at the end of each verse)*

Oh, let's pretend! Yes, let's
   pretend
That we are something new.
Let's pretend we're lots of
   things
And see what we can do.

David is a cowboy,
Riding up a hill,              *(Ride pony)*
Until his pony stumbles
And David takes a spill.     *(Fall down)*

Jeannie is an autumn leaf.
She twirls and twirls around.   *(Dance with many turns)*
She twists and turns and
   twirls again,
And tumbles to the ground.   *(Fall down)*

Kathy is a candle straight.   *(Stand tall and straight)*
Too bad! She got too hot.
She's bending almost double,  *(Bend 'way over)*
Something like a knot.

Kevin is an airplane
Flying high and grand,
Until he sees an airport
Where he has to land.

*(Extend arms and glide around room)*
*(Bend knees until extended arms touch floor)*

Sally is a firefly,
Flitting in the night;
Until the morning comes
And she puts out her light.

*(Dance with jerky motions)*

*(Kneel down and curl up)*

Kenny is a snowman
Who smiles and looks around
Until the sun smiles back at him
And he melts to the ground.

*(Stand still and smile)*

*(Gradually kneel as if melting)*

What else can you pretend?
What do other people do?
If you will act it out,
I'll try to do it, too.

—BERNICE WELLS CARLSON

## MONKEY SHINES

I had a little monkey.
He learned to climb a string.    (*Climb hand-over-hand. Get on*
He learned to climb a tree.      *your tiptoes and stretch*)
He climbed most everything!

One night he climbed a
    moonbeam,
Until he reached the sky.
He grabbed the nearest star      (*Extend left arm. Clench fist.*
    point.                            *Wave with right hand*)
The moon was floating by.

"It's chilly on your moon-
    beam.
Excuse me! I must sneeze."       (*Make sneezing sound. Cover*
"God bless you!" said the        *mouth with right hand. Con-*
    moon man.                         *tinue to hang with left*)
"Have some of my green
    cheese."

"No, thank you," said the
    monkey.                           (*Wave, "No," with right hand.*
"I don't like the smell."        *Hold nose with left*)
He let go of the star point      (*Fall down*)
And down to earth he fell.       (*Keep slumping*)

Pell mell! Oh, well!
Monkeys don't belong on
    moonbeams, do they?

—BERNICE WELLS CARLSON

ACTION STORIES

## ACTION STORIES

Act-out stories may be used to teach and entertain one child or a group. If they are to have fun, children must listen and follow directions. This type of story gives children an opportunity to let off steam and to do vigorous exercises under controlled conditions. Most children find the stories, and the action, more enjoyable and more interesting than calisthenics. One important feature is that the stories all end quietly.

Test the listeners' ability to follow directions. Don't tell or read a story until children follow perfectly your signal to be quiet. As a simple test, ask them to clap and then to stop when you raise your hand.

Know the story well enough so that you, too, can act it out as you tell it. If you must read it, rather than tell it from memory, be so familiar with it that you need look at the book only now and then. The children respond at the right time by listening to your voice and watching your directions. In most stories you can change the actions to include many exercises which that child or group particularly needs.

Encourage children to tell these stories or make up similar stories. Insist on the one rule: Stories must end quietly.

# THE SPACEMAN IN THE ROCKET SHIP

(*Do what the Spaceman does*)

One day a Spaceman landed in our back yard. He was sitting in a rocket ship that looked very much like a rock, a rock from your garden or a rock from the mountains on the moon. The Spaceman was cramped in his rocket ship. He sat all squeezed up. (*Sit squeezed up*)

"Mmmmm—" he thought. "I wonder where I am. I had better find out."

The Spaceman stood up. (*Stand up*) He stretched his arms. (*Stretch arms*) He stretched his legs. (*Stretch up on tiptoes, with arms extended*) He pulled up his antennae. (*Pull up imaginary antennae*) When he pulled up his antennae, he got a message. "This is earth."

"Earth?" said the Spaceman, settling back on his heels. (*Stand straight*) "Earth! I think I like earth. It has oxygen." He took three deep breaths. (*Take three deep breaths*)

"Mmmmm," said the Spaceman. "Oxygen makes me feel vigorous." He raised his arms and twirled them around and around. (*Raise arms shoulder height and twirl them around*) He twisted his body back and forth. (*With arms still extended, twist trunk of body*) He leaned over and touched his shoes. (*Lean over and touch shoes*) He stood up straight. (*Stand straight*) He lifted his knees, one, two, three, four. (*Lift knees*) He jumped into the air and clapped his hands. (*Jump into air and clap hands*)

Then he stood still and looked up, and to the left, and to the right. (*Stand still, look up, left and right*) He turned around. (*Turn around*)

Everywhere he looked he saw children.

He heard them say, "Look at that queer bug! Let's catch it."

"Yes, let's catch it. Let's use it for 'Show and Tell.' "

"Let's put it on the science table."

"Let's make a project for the science fair."

The Spaceman didn't understand about "show and tell," or a science table, or a science fair. He was frightened, so frightened that he slipped quietly into his space rocket. (*Slide into seat. Sit quietly*) He pulled in his antennae. (*Pull in imaginary antennae*) He didn't want to hear any more about "show and tell," or a science table, or a project for a science fair.

The children stopped talking and looked for their spaceman. But they couldn't find him because he was in his space rocket. The space rocket looked just like a rock, a rock from your garden, or maybe a rock from the mountains on the moon.

—BERNICE WELLS CARLSON

## JUST LIKE BROWNIE

*(Do what Brownie does. Brownie does things a little faster each day)*

Once upon a time, a Brownie came to live in Jimmy's house. He thought, "I'd like to do what Jimmy does; but I can't learn everything at once. Each day I'll do one new thing."

On Monday, when the alarm went off, Brownie jumped out of bed and washed his hands and face at 7:30 in the morning. (*Jump, wash hands and face. Sit down*)

On Tuesday, when the alarm went off, Brownie jumped out of bed, washed his hands and face, and brushed his teeth at 7:30 in the morning. (*Jump up, wash hands and face, brush teeth. Sit down*)

On Wednesday, when the alarm went off, Brownie jumped out

of bed, washed his hands and face, brushed his teeth, and dressed himself at 7:30 in the morning. (*Wash hands and face, brush teeth, dress self. Sit down*)

On Thursday, when the alarm went off, Brownie jumped out of bed, washed his hands and face, brushed his teeth, dressed himself, and ate breakfast. (*Wash hands and face, brush teeth, dress self, eat breakfast. Sit down*)

On Friday, when the alarm went off, Brownie jumped out of bed, washed his hands and face, brushed his teeth, dressed himself, ate his breakfast, and waved good-bye to Jimmy's daddy who was on his way to work at 7:30 in the morning. (*Very rapidly, wash hands and face, brush teeth, dress self, eat breakfast, and wave good-bye. Sit down*)

On Saturday, when the alarm went off, Brownie turned over and shut it off. (*Move right arm across body slowly, as if shutting off an alarm*) He had heard Jimmy say, "This is Saturday. Nobody gets up at 7:30 in the morning on Saturday!"

(You can make up your own Brownie stories, based on things you like to do. Always end with something quiet. For example Brownie can go to the playground and use a new piece of equipment each day, until he finds a tree. He sits down and goes to sleep under a tree. He can do a new exercise each day. The last exercise is to sit very straight and very still. Brownie can go to visit Grandpa on the farm. He can do one new thing each day, until he discovers Grandpa's old rocker. He just sits there and rocks and rocks until he is tired of rocking.)

—BERNICE WELLS CARLSON

71

## SENSIBLE, QUIET CLIFFORD JONES

*(Do what Clifford Jones does. Do not do what the other children do)*

Clifford Jones went to a Christmas party at the club. He hoped that the chairman would choose him to be first to shake hands with Santa Claus.

Clifford Jones sat in the chair where he was supposed to sit. *(Sit up straight)* He folded his hands and looked around. *(Fold hands. Look around)* No one paid any attention to Clifford Jones.

So Clifford Jones stood up. *(Stand up)* He stretched his neck, looking one way and then another. *(Stretch, looking one way and then the other)* No one paid any attention to Clifford Jones.

Then Clifford Jones raised his right hand very high. *(Raise right hand high)* He raised his left hand high. *(Raise left hand high)* He waved both hands up high. *(Wave both hands high in air)* He bent his arms and twisted back and forth. *(Bend arms. Twist back and forth)* No one paid any attention to Clifford Jones.

Then Clifford Jones put his hands near his face and made a lot of silly motions and silly faces. *(Make silly motions with hands and silly faces)* No one paid any attention to Clifford Jones.

Clifford Jones was tired. He sat down. *(Sit down)* He folded his hands in his lap. *(Fold hands in lap)* He sat quietly. *(Sit quietly)*

Just then Santa Claus entered the room saying, "Ho! Ho! Ho!" Most of the children stood up and waved and wiggled. But Clifford Jones sat still with his hands in his lap. He looked, and looked, and looked at Santa Claus. *(Sit still with hands in lap, looking straight ahead)*

72

Santa and the chairman motioned for the children to sit down and be quiet. Then Santa asked, "Who is that boy sitting there so quietly with his hands folded in his lap?"

"That's Clifford Jones," said the chairman.

"Clifford Jones," repeated Santa Claus. "Mmmmm— Clifford Jones looks like a quiet sensible boy. I'd like to shake his hand and give him the first gift."

Everybody paid attention then to Clifford Jones, quiet sensible Clifford Jones, when Santa shook his hand and gave him the first gift.

—BERNICE WELLS CARLSON

## THE QUOCKERMONGER

*(Do as the Quockermonger does and join him in saying, "Yakitty, yakitty, yak, yak, yak!)*

Did you ever see a Quockermonger? No? Well, there's a good reason. He's obsolete. That means he's not used any more. Not anyone I know talks about a Quockermonger.

But there was a time when young folks, old folks, rich folks, poor folks, everyone, went to Quockermonger shows. A Quockermonger was a special kind of puppet with a wooden head. Like some foolish people he did a lot of things but never thought at all.

He shook his fists. (*Shake fists*)
Raised his arms up high. (*Raise arms*)
Swung his arms back and forth. (*Swing arms*)
Moved his body left and right. (*Sway torso left and right*)
Stamped his feet. (*Stamp feet*)

Pounded on the table. (*Pound table*)

"Looks as if he is making a speech," people said, "but he doesn't say anything."

So one puppeteer gave his Quockermonger a mouth that could open. It said one thing, "*Yakitty, yakitty, yak, yak, yak!*"

Soon every Quockermonger had a mouth that could open. Every mouth said the same thing, "*Yakitty, yakitty, yak, yak, yak!*"

So then, when the puppeteer gave a show, the Quockermonger:

Shook his fists. (*Shake fists*) And said, "*Yakitty, yakitty, yak, yak, yak!*"

Raised his arms up. (*Raise arms*) And said, "*Yakitty, yakitty, yak, yak, yak!*"

Swung his arms back and forth. (*Swing arms*) And said, "*Yakitty, yakitty, yak, yak, yak!*"

Moved his body left and right. (*Sway torso left and right*) And said, "*Yakitty, yakitty, yak yak, yak!*"

Stamped his feet. (*Stamp feet*) And said, "*Yakitty, yakitty, yak, yak, yak!*"

Pounded on the table. (*Pound table*) And said, "*Yakitty, yakitty, yak, yak, yak! Yakitty, yakitty, yak, yak, yak! Yakitty, yakitty, yak, yak, yak!*"

Folks got tired of the Quockermonger. They didn't go to the Quockermonger shows. They forgot about the Quockermonger. He became obsolete—not used any more. Can you guess why?

—BERNICE WELLS CARLSON

*A quockermonger is a puppet, or "a politician acting under an outsider's order."*

# POEMS WITH
# SOUND EFFECTS

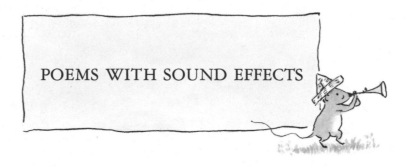

# POEMS WITH SOUND EFFECTS

Each verse of these poems ends with a sound effect which the child is expected to make with you at the right time. If it is a prolonged sound, such as *Shhhhh,* raise your hand when it is time to stop. Making sounds of this type, and blowing, help to develop breath control, a very important prerequisite for speech development.

In some cases the sound effect is made in different ways. For example, a kitten *mee-ows* one way when it is happy and another way when it is sad. The child must listen to the verse to determine how the sound effect should be made. An early start in dramatics comes of listening and then making a noise at the right time, in keeping with the mood of the character of the story.

Activities of this kind help to increase a child's attention span. He must wait and listen until it is time to make a response.

These verses can be fun in ways other than reading. They can provide an opportunity for verbal communication when an adult and a child want to talk, and the child doesn't have much to say. If you learn a few verses, which you no doubt will do automatically after reading them more than once, you can recite them in many impromptu situations when you are doing tasks that require little concentration, such as walking to the store with a child, or doing routine household chores while he is in the room and seems to be looking for something to do. For example, if you recite a verse of "Two Little Kittens Who Had a Fight," the child may respond "Me-ow, me-ow! Me-ow, me-ow! Ffffft!" Or you may see or hear something that reminds you both of a verse. If a child sees a big fly, he may say, *"Buzz,"* and you may respond, *" 'Hmmm,' said the bee."* Together you may say, *"Buzz, Hmmm! Buzz, Hmmm!"* as in the little verse. In this way, the verse becomes a game for two people who have shared a reading experience.

## BABY SLEEPS AT HOME

*(At the end of each verse, say "Shhhh—")*

Hush, the waves are rolling in,
White with foam; white with foam.
Father toils amidst the din;
But baby sleeps at home. *Shhhh—*

Hush, the winds roar hoarse and deep.
On they come! On they come!
Brother keeps the wandering sheep;
But baby sleeps at home. *Shhhh—*

Hush, the rain sweeps o'er the meadows,
Where they roam; where they roam.
Sister goes to seek the cows;
But baby sleeps at home. *Shhhh—*

—ADAPTED FROM OLD GAELIC LULLABY
AUTHOR UNKNOWN

## BUZZ, HMMMMM

(*At the end of the verse, make the noise of the fly and the bee flying together*)

"*Buzz*," says the blue fly.
"*Hmmm*," says the bee,
"*Buzz*," and "*Hmmm*," they cry,
And so do we.
*Buzz, Hmmm! Buzz, Hmmm!*
*Buzz, Hmmm, Buzz!*

—ADAPTED FROM AN OLD RHYME

## THE NORTH WIND

(*Moan like the north wind at the end of the verse*)

The north wind blew.
It rattled the windows.
It swept down the flue.
The great trees groaned,
As the north wind moaned.
*Owwwwww! Owwwwww!*
*Owwwwww!*

—AUTHOR UNKNOWN

82

## THE CHEE-CHOO BIRD

*(Say chee-choo at the end of each line as you think the bird would say it)*

A little green bird sat on a
    fence rail.
Chee-choo, chee-choo, chee-    *(Happily)*
    choo!

The song was the sweetest I
    ever heard.
Chee-choo, chee-choo, chee-    *(Happily)*
    choo!

I ran for some salt to put on
    his tail.
Chee-choo, chee-choo, chee-    *(Suspiciously)*
    choo!

But while I was gone, away
    flew the bird.
Chee-choo, chee-choo, chee-    *(Quickly and happily)*
    choo!

—AUTHOR UNKNOWN

## THE WITCH ON A WINDY NIGHT

*(At the end of a verse move your finger in a big circle and say together, "Shuuuuuuuuuuuu")*

An old witch sat at home all alone;
Cooking and cooking a big soup bone.
And the wind blew all around the house.     *Shuuuuuuuuuuuu!*

"Oh, who will share my soup," she crowed.
"If I drink it all, I'll surely explode!"
And the wind blew all around the house.     *Shuuuuuuuuuuuu!*

A big dog barked at her front door;
"Go away!" she said. "I chased you before!"
And the wind blew all around the house.     *Shuuuuuuuuuuuu!*

"Oh, will you share your soup with me?"
The black cat purred, "With me? With me?"
And the wind blew all around the house.     *Shuuuuuuuuuuuu!*

"I've changed my mind! I hate to share!"
"Let everyone starve for all I care!"
And the wind blew all around the house.     *Shuuuuuuuuuuuu!*

"I'll drink the soup myself!" she sang.
What happened then? She exploded. Bang!
And the wind blew all around the house.     *Shuuuuuuuuuuuu!*

—BERNICE WELLS CARLSON (*Play Activities for the Retarded Child by Bernice Wells Carlson and David R. Ginglend*)

# THERE WAS AN OLD WOMAN

*(At the end of each verse join the old woman in talking, saying only "Chatter, chatter, chatter." At the end of the second verse show surprise in the way you chatter)*

There was an old woman, and what do you think?
She lived upon nothing but victuals and drink.
Victuals and drink were the chief of her diet
Yet this plaguey old woman would never keep quiet.
*Chatter, chatter, chatter! Chatter, chatter, chatter!*

She went to the baker's to buy some bread,
And when she got back her poor husband was dead.
She went to the clerk's to toll the great bell,
And when she came back her husband was well.
*Chatter, chatter, chatter! Chatter, chatter, chatter!*

—W. W. GILCHRIST

## TWO LITTLE KITTENS WHO HAD A FIGHT

(*After each verse make the sounds the kittens make in the way you think they would make them*)

Two little kittens one stormy night
Began to quarrel and then to fight.
One had a mouse, the other had none;
That was the way the fight had begun.
"Me-ow, me-ow! Me-ow, me-ow! Ffffft!"  (*Angry*)

"I'll have that mouse," said the bigger cat.
*"You'll* have it? We'll see about that!"
"I will have the mouse!" said the older son.
"You shan't have that mouse," said the little one.
"Me-ow, me-ow! Me-ow, me-ow! Fffft!"          (*Much angrier*)

I told you before, 'twas a stormy night,
When these two kittens began to fight.
The old woman seized her sweeping broom,
And swept both kittens right out of the room.
"Me-ow, me-ow! Me-ow, me-ow! Meee-ow!"          (*Surprised*)

The ground was covered with frost and snow;
The two little kittens had nowhere to go.
They snuggled down on the mat by the door,
And cried that they never would fight anymore.
"Me-ow, me-ow! Me-ow, me-ow! Meee-ooow!"          (*Crying*)

Then they both crept in as quiet as mice,
All wet with snow and as cold as ice.
They found it better—I'm sure they were right—
To lie down and sleep than to quarrel and fight.
"Me-ow, me-ow. Me-ow, me-ow. Prrrrrrrr."          (*Slowly and
contentedly*)

—ADAPTED. AUTHOR UNKNOWN

## HEAR MY FEET WHEN I GO OUT

*(In this poem are the different sounds a child makes with his feet when he goes out of doors in different seasons. Encourage him to make these sounds with you, especially when they are repeated in the last line)*

In summer I go out.
I splash in water from the hose.
Hear it splashing on my toes!
*Swish, swosh, swish, swosh.*
Hear me splashing near the hose!
*Swish, swosh, swish, swosh.*

In autumn I go out.
I shuffle through the golden leaves
That have fallen from the trees.
*Crinkle, crackle, crinkle, crackle.*
Hear me shuffle through the leaves!
*Crinkle, crackle, crinkle, crackle.*

In winter I go out.
I tramp and break the crusty snow.
Hear me tramping to and fro!
*Creak, squeak, creak, squeak.*
Hear me tramping on the snow!
*Creak, squeak, creak, squeak.*

In spring I go out.
I step or stomp in every puddle.
See it ooze! See it bubble!
*Squish, squash, squish, squash.*
Hear me wading in the puddle!
*Squish, squash, squish, squash—PLUNK!*
Hear me falling in the puddle?
I fell down. What a mess!

—BERNICE WELLS CARLSON

## THE YOUNG MUSICIAN

(*At the end of each verse, make the noise that the instrument is making. At first, tap with your finger eight times to get the rhythm. Later pretend to play the instruments in time to the sounds. See other suggestions on page 91*)

Oh, I'm a young musician;
From distant lands I come.
Singing and playing,
Ever I'm straying.
My fiddle is saying,
*Simm, Simm! Simm, Simm!*
*Simm, Simm! Simm, Simm!*

Oh, I'm a young musician;
From distant lands I come.
Singing and playing,
Ever I'm straying.
My trombone is saying,
*Pom, Pom! Pom, Pom!*
*Pom, Pom! Pom, Pom!*

Oh, I'm a young musician;
From distant lands I come.
Singing and playing,
Ever I'm straying.
My bass drum is saying,
*Drom, Drom! Drom, Drom!*     (*Roll r Drrr-om*)
*Drom, Drom! Drom, Drom!*

—GERMAN AND DANISH FOLKSONG

(If you are working with a group of children, divide them into three groups. Use "We" rather than "I" in the verse. At the end of the first verse, the first group plays like a fiddle, *Simm, Simm!* At the end of the second verse, the second group plays like the trombone, *Pom, Pom!* and the fiddle group plays *Simm, Simm!* At the end of the third verse, the third group plays like a drum, *Drom, Drom!* while the trombone group plays *Pom, Pom!* and the fiddle group plays, *Simm, Simm!*)

## A SPANISH BALLAD

(*Listen to the sound of the guitar and at the end of each verse. Repeat it*)

A gentleman in fair Madrid,
He loved a lovely maid; he did;
Of all the maids, the pearl, the pink,
*Oh, tink-a-tink-a-tink-a-tink!*
*Oh, tink-a-tink-a-tink-a-tink!*

He followed her both near and far,
Performing on his light guitar,
And often at her feet he sank,
*Oh, tank-a-tank-a-tank-a-tank!*
*Oh, tank-a-tank-a-tank-a-tank!*

But she remained both grim and grave,
"I wish," she said, "you would behave!"
And so he went and was a monk.
*Oh, tunk-a-tunk-a-tunk-a-tunk!*
*Oh, tunk-a-tunk-a-tunk-a-tunk!*

—CAROLINE M. FULLER

## ON MUSIC THEY DOTE

(At the end of each limerick, the singer sings the scale in his own way—the lion, *Grrrrrrr!* The mouse, *Sque-e-e-eak!* The cat, *Mee-ou-ou-ou-ou-ou-ouw!* The dame, *Do-re-mi-fa-sol-la-ti-do!* Sing each scale as the character would sing it)

Said the lion:   "On music I dote
But something is wrong with my throat.
When I practice a scale,
The listeners quail
And flee at the very first note.
Gr-rr-rr-rr-rr-rr-rr-rr!"     (*Do re mi fa sol la ti do* as the *lion would sing it*)

Said the mouse: "I like popular hits
But I can't find a tune that just fits.
When I sing women scream
And go off the beam
As if they had lost half their wits.
Sque-e-e-e-e-e-e-eak!"     (*The scale as the mouse would sing it*)

Said the cat:   "I sing best in the night
When the moon is beautifully bright;
But folks seldom care.
Old shoes fill the air,
Till I stop my nighttime delight.
Me-ou-ou-ou-ou-ou-ou-ouw!"   (*The scale as
the cat would sing it*)

Said the dame:   "To opera I do aspire.
Untold practice the art does require;
So plug up your ears,
And calm all your fears—
One more scale and then I'll retire.
Do, re, mi, fa, sol, la, ti, do!"

—ADAPTED BY BERNICE WELLS CARLSON FROM A VERSE BY OLIVER HERFORD

## WHIMPEY, LITTLE WHIMPEY

*(At the end of each verse, cry like Little Whimpey, until the last verse)*

Whimpey, little Whimpey,
  Cried so much one day,
His Grandma couldn't stand it,
  And his Mother ran away.
His Sister climbed the hay mow.
  His Father went to town.
The Cook flew to the neighbor's
  In her shabby gown.
*Boo-hoo! Boo-hoo! Boo-hoo!*

Whimpey, little Whimpey,
  Stood out in the sun,
And cried until the chickens
  And ducks began to run.
Old Towser in his kennel
  Growled in an angry tone,
Then burst his chain, and Whimpey
  Was left standing there alone!
*Boo-hoo! Boo-hoo! Boo-hoo!*

Whimpey, little Whimpey,
  Cried and cried and cried.
Soon the sunlight vanished;
  Flowers began to hide;
Birdies stopped their singing;
  Frogs began to croak.
Darkness came and Whimpey
  Found crying was no joke.
*Boo-hoo! Boo-hoo! Boo-hoo!*

Whimpey, little Whimpey,
  Ne'er'll forget the day,
When Grandma couldn't stand it
  And his Mother ran away.
He was waiting by the window
  When they came home to tea,
And a gladder boy than Whimpey,
  You need never hope to see.
*Hooray! Hooray! Hooray!*

—ADAPTED. AUTHOR UNKNOWN

## JEFF BROWN HAD A GRAY MULE

*(Make the noise of the gray mule at the end of each verse. If you wish, put your hands at the sides of your head with fingers sticking up, like ears. Lower and raise your fingers as you say, "He-haw!")*

Jeff Brown had a little gray mule.
  *He-haw, he-haw, he-haw!*
Its ears were long. It looked like a fool.
  *He-haw, he-haw, he-haw!*
Jeff Brown was riding up Shuter's bank.
  *He-haw, he-haw, he-haw!*
The old gray mule did kick and prank,
  *He-haw, he-haw, he-haw!*
Jeff Brown was riding up Shuter's hill.
  *He-haw, he-haw, he-haw!*
His mule fell down. Jeff took a spill.
  *He-haw, he-haw, he-haw!*
The bridle and saddle are now on the shelf.
  *He-haw, he-haw, he-haw!*
If you want any more you can sing it yourself.
  *He-haw, he-haw, he-haw!*

—BASED ON OLD ENGLISH RHYME

# STORIES WITH
# SOUND EFFECTS

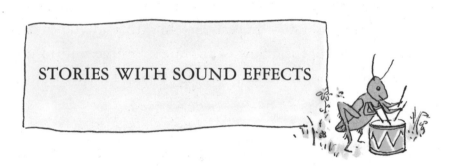

# STORIES WITH SOUND EFFECTS

The child is expected to join you in making the right sounds at the proper places in the stories. He must listen intently to do this for the sounds occur at irregular intervals and there is no rhyme or meter, as in a poem, to prompt a response.

The sound should be made as the character in the story would make it and as the mood indicates. For example, a happy cricket chirps in a different way than a disappointed cricket chirps. To catch this difference, a child must listen, think, and interpret—a big order!

Practice the sounds at least once before you read or tell the story to the child. If he suggests sounds other than those given here, accept his ideas. In one of the stories in this section, a child is asked to suggest sounds. If he doesn't know how something sounds, help him. Tell him, for example, that a paddle boat on a river goes *Slash, slash.*"

In the case of a prolonged sound, such as a drill going *brrrr,* raise your hand when it is time to stop. The child will learn to follow both your auditory and visual commands. This is especially important when working with a group of young children.

Read the story, pausing only briefly for the sound effect which is printed in italics. Expect the child to join you in saying it, but don't interrupt the flow of the story to urge him to take part. He will join you in making the right sound at the right time when he is ready to do so.

# THE NICEST PLACE IN THE WORLD

(*In this story little Otto hears animal and bird noises. Your child-listener makes the noises. When, for example, you have said, "The little mouse said . . ." the child responds, "Squeak, squeak." At the proper place the child says, for the little chick, "Peep, peep," and responds with the proper sounds for all the animals and birds throughout the story.*)

Little Otto was thinking. He was thinking that he wanted to live in the nicest place in the world.

"Where is the nicest place in the world?" he asked himself. Everyone around him was much too busy to answer, so he went up to the attic. An attic is a good place to sit and think. Just as he sat down to think, he saw a mouse.

"Pardon me, Little Mouse," said Little Otto. "Can you tell me the nicest place in the world to live?"

The Little Mouse said, *"Squeak, squeak!* The nicest place in the world to live is in a hole." Without making another sound, the little mouse darted into a hole in the side of the wall.

Little Otto got down on his hands and knees and looked into the hole. "A hole may be a very good home for a mouse," said Little Otto, "but I don't want to live in a hole in the wall."

Little Otto went down the stairs, out of the house, and into the barn. A barn is a good place to sit and think. Just as he started to sit down, he saw a little chick.

"Pardon me, Little Chick," said Little Otto. "Can you tell me the nicest place in the world to live?"

The Little Chick said, *"Peep, peep!* The nicest place in the world to live is under the wing of a mother hen." Without making another sound, the little chick crept under the wing of the mother hen.

Little Otto started to lift the wing of the mother hen, but she pecked him very hard!

"Well," said Little Otto, drawing back. "Under the wing of a mother hen may be a good place for a chick to live, but I don't want to live under the wing of a mother hen."

Little Otto went into the woods. A woods is a good place to sit and think. Before he could sit down, he saw a robin.

"Pardon me, Mother Robin," said Little Otto. "Can you tell me the nicest place in the world to live?"

Mother Robin said, *"Cheer-up, cheer-up!* The nicest place in the world to live is in a nest."

Little Otto tried to climb the tree to reach the nest, but he couldn't get his feet off the ground.

"Well," said Little Otto. "A nest may be a very good place for a robin to live, but I don't want to live in a nest!"

Just then Little Otto heard an old owl say, *"Oooooo!* I know the nicest place in the world to live."

"Don't tell me it's a hole in a tree!" said Little Otto, who had suddenly really started to think.

The old owl said, *"Oooooo!* The nicest place in the world to live is in your own home."

"That's right!" said Little Otto. "Thank you, Mr. Owl."

Little Otto ran home as fast as he could, up the steps of the porch, and into the kichen where his mother was working.

"Mother," said Little Otto, "I know the nicest place in the world to live."

His mother said, *"Oh?"*

"I know the nicest place in the world to live," said Little Otto. "Right here!"

—BERNICE WELLS CARLSON

# WHAT WAS BEHIND THE DOOR?

*(In this story, you make the animal noises which Granny hears. When the story says, "Granny heard a dog say," you say, "Bow-wow!" "Granny heard a cat say," you say, "Mee-ow, mee-ow!" "Granny heard a bird say," you say, "Peep, peep!" "Granny heard a lion say," you say, "Grrrrr!" Listen carefully and make the noises at the right time)*

Granny sat in a big armchair mending Tommy's socks. All of a sudden she heard a dog say, *"Bow-wow!"*

"Gracious!" said Granny. "I do believe there's a dog behind the door. Should we have a dog in the house?"

"Oh, yes," answered the dog behind the door. "I'm a good dog. I don't jump at people."

"Very well," said Granny, and she went on darning socks for Tommy. All of a sudden Granny heard a cat say, *"Mee-ow, mee-ow!"*

"Gracious!" said Granny. "I do believe there is a cat behind the door. Should we have a cat in the house?"

"Oh, yes," answered the cat. "I am a good cat. I do not scratch the rug."

"Very well," said Granny, and she went on darning Tommy's socks. All of a sudden Granny heard a bird say, *"Peep, peep!"*

"Gracious!" said Granny. "I do believe there is a bird behind the door. Should we have a bird in the house?"

"Oh, yes," answered the bird. "I am a good bird. I sing sweetly."

"Very well," said Granny, and she went right on darning

Tommy's socks. All of a sudden Granny heard a lion say, *"Grrrrr!"*

"Gracious!" said Granny. "I do believe there is a lion behind the door. This is too much!"

Granny put down her darning. She stood up. She looked behind the door. What do you think she saw?

Of course it was Tommy! You knew it all the time, didn't you?

—BERNICE WELLS CARLSON

## THE CRICKET IN THE PALACE

*(In this story the cricket says, "Chirp-chirp! Chirp-chirp!" When you have read or said, "The cricket said," the child makes the sound in the way he thinks the cricket would say it, happily, angrily, or sadly)*

Once upon a time, long long ago, there lived in the fields outside the palace gate a little cricket. All summer long he sang happily, *"Chirp-chirp! Chirp-chirp!"*

When the autumn winds began to blow, the cricket began to shiver, saying, *"Chirp-chirp! Chirp-chirp!"*

"I must find a warmer place to live," he told himself. So he stretched his six little legs, and half walking, half hopping, he went out of the field, down the cobblestone walk, across the drawbridge, and through the palace door.

There in the great hall, stood a palace guard, stiff as a statue. Wishing to be friendly, the little cricket said, *"Chirp-chirp! Chirp-chirp!"*

The guard looked straight ahead, never moving a muscle.

"Too bad he doesn't hear well," thought the little cricket. "I'll get closer to his ear." So, wishing to be friendly, the little cricket climbed up the long silk stocking of the guard, up his shiny black trousers, up his elegant coat, up the stiff white ruff around the neck, up to the ear of the guard who stood still as a statue. Then the little cricket spoke more loudly, saying, *"Chirp-chirp! Chirp-chirp!"*

"Get out of the way, you spider!" said the guard without looking. With his hand, he brushed the cricket onto the floor.

Spider? A cricket isn't a spider! No cricket likes to be brushed upon the floor. The little cricket said, angrily, *"Chirp-chirp! Chirp-chirp!"*

Then he thought, "Perhaps the guard doesn't know much about crickets. I'll forgive him." The little cricket picked himself up on his six legs and, half walking, half hopping, went into a sunny room where a pinched-in maid was mending a royal petticoat.

"She looks lonely," thought the little cricket. "I'll go close, where she can see me." So, wishing to be friendly, the little cricket crawled slowly up the royal petticoat the maid was mending, across the lap of the maid, up the petticoat again. He rested on top of the finger that was holding the cloth. Then the cricket said merrily, *"Chirp-chirp! Chirp-chirp!"*

The pinched-in maid squinted at the cricket on her finger and screamed, "Get out of the way, you beetle!" She shook the royal petticoat and dumped the cricket onto the floor.

Beetle? A cricket isn't a beetle! No cricket likes to be dumped onto the floor. The cricket said angrily, *"Chirp-chirp! Chirp-chirp!"*

Then he thought, "Perhaps the pinched-in maid doesn't know much about crickets. I'll forgive her." He picked himself up on his six little legs and, half walking, half hopping, went down the hall and into the warmest room in the palace—the kitchen. Near the work table stood a healthy-looking cook, peeling potatoes.

"Oh," thought the cricket, "I'd like to live with the cook in this big warm kitchen." So, wishing to be friendly, he hopped up on the work table and said, cheerily, *"Chirp-chirp! Chirp-chirp!"*

The healthy-looking cook looked at the cricket on her work table and scolded, "Get out of the way, you waterbug!" With one stroke of her big wet hand, she swished the cricket onto the floor.

Waterbug? A cricket isn't a waterbug! No cricket likes to be swished upon the floor. The cricket said, angrily, *"Chirp-chirp! Chirp-chirp!"*

Then he thought, "Perhaps the cook doesn't know much about crickets. I'll forgive her." He picked himself up on his six legs and hopped up the stairs of the palace. He heard someone singing.

"I love my clown
   And my clown loves me."

He looked into the room. There sat the little Princess, bouncing her jester doll on her knee. As she bounced her doll, she sang a song, which she must have made up herself.

"I love my clown

And my clown loves me.

We live together

So happily."

"That's a good song," thought the cricket, "but it needs a chorus." He hopped very quietly across the floor, up a table leg, and onto the arm of the chair in which the Princess was sitting. This time when the Princess sang her song, he added a chorus, saying, *"Chirp-chirp! Chirp-chirp!"*

"Oh, you precious little cricket!" said the Princess. "You sing very sweetly, but you don't belong on my chair." With great care, the Princess picked up the little cricket and placed him gently on the hearth where it was snug and warm.

"There," said the Princess. "You can stay on the hearth. When I sing to my doll you can sing with me."

The cricket said, *"Chirp-chirp! Chirp-chirp!"* meaning, of course, "That's a good idea!"

During all that winter, the people who lived in the palace often heard a new song—a song with a chorus. It went like this:

"I love my clown,

And my clown loves me.

We live together,

So happily.

*Chirp-chirp! Chirp-chirp!*

*Chirp-chirp! Chirp-chirp!"*

—BERNICE WELLS CARLSON

111

## CHUG-ALONG AND ZOOM

*(In this story the old car says, "Chug-along, chug-along, chug, chug, chug." The new car says, "Zoom!" When the story says, "The old car said," make the sound of the old car. When the story says, "The new car said," make that sound. Change the speed with which you make the sound according to what is happening in the story)*

Once there was a very old car. When it went down the road it said, *"Chug-along, chug-along, chug, chug, chug."* There was also a new car. When it went down the road it said, *"Zoom!"*

Every day the old car went down Skillmans' Lane. When it went up the hill it said slowly, *"Chug-along, chug-along, chug, chug, chug."* When it went down a hill it said, a little faster, *"Chug-along, chug-along, chug, chug, chug."*

Every day the new car went down Skillmans' Lane. When it went up a hill it said fast, *"Zoom!"* When it went down a hill it said fast, *"Zoom!"* It always went as fast as the law allowed.

Every day the new car and the old car parked side by side in a company parking lot.

"You go too fast on Skillmans' Lane," commented the old car one day when work was over. "Skillmans' Lane is very bumpy. Skillmans' Lane has many curves. You should slow down on Skillmans' Lane."

"Axle grease!" sneered the new car. "I am a new car. You are an old car. I can take bumps. I can take curves. I like to go as fast as the law allows. Good-bye now!" He left the parking lot saying, *"Zoom!"*

"Good-bye," called the old car. He left the parking lot saying, *"Chug-along, chug-along, chug, chug, chug."*

Now Skillmans' Lane was a country road. It was always bumpy. In summer and fall it was bumpy and dusty. In winter it was bumpy and snowy. In spring it was bumpy and muddy—very, very muddy, slishy, slashy, slide-around muddy—and it was full of holes.

In the spring the old car went down Skillmans' Lane very carefully, dodging holes, going slowly over the bumps, and making sure not to get its wheels in the soft mud at the side of the road. It kept saying, *"Chug-along, chug-along, chug, chug, chug."*

The new car paid no attention to the mud. It went up the hill saying, *"Zoom!"* It started down the hill saying, *"Zoom—Bang!"* It hit a bump, swerved into the mud, and slid into a tree.

The old car heard the crash. It hurried up the hill as fast as it could go safely saying, *"Chug-along, chug-along, chug, chug, chug."*

"Stay where you are," called the old car. "I'll get a wrecker to pull you out." Off he went saying, *"Chug-along, chug-along, chug, chug, chug."*

The wrecker pulled the new car onto the road. It was a sad sight. It was all covered with mud; its headlights were broken; its fenders were bent. However, its engine was still running. "Oh, thank you, little old car. Thank you, wrecker. I think I can go on." He started down the road saying, slowly, *"Z-o-o-m."*

The cars still go down Skillmans' Lane. The old car says, *"Chug-along, chug-along, chug, chug, chug."* Sometimes it goes very slowly saying, *"Chug-along, chug-along, chug, chug, chug."* Sometimes it goes a little faster saying, *"Chug-along, chug-along, chug, chug, chug."* It all depends upon the condition of the road.

The nearly new car goes down Skillmans' Lane. Sometimes it goes very slowly saying, *"Z-o-o-m."* Sometimes it goes a little faster saying, *"Zoom!"* Everything depends upon the condition of the road.

—BERNICE WELLS CARLSON (*The Party Book for Boys and Girls*)

## ONE EGG? TWO EGGS?

*(Some sounds are very much the same, no matter where you hear them. People in other parts of the world interpret them a little differently than we do, however. The Japanese say that a happy dog barks, "Wan-wan! Wan-wan-wan!" A laying hen cackles, "Koke-ko-ko!" A soft wind whispers, "Zawa, zawa, zawa." A cat purrs, "Goro, goro, goro."*

*In this story, which is part of a longer story, you will hear these noises, and some sounds you don't hear in your own home. When the story says, "The gentle wind says," you say, "Zawa, zawa, zawa." When the story says, "The cat purrs," you say, "Goro, goro, goro." Try to remember also the other Japanese sounds)*

Sachi was a Japanese girl who lived on a little farm with her father, her mother, and her brother. She was like other Japanese girls in almost every way, but in one way she was different. Sachi was blind.

Instead of living in a world full of shapes, color, and movement, Sachi lived in a world where she could enjoy only the sense of touch, of taste, of smell, and of sound. How she loved to feel the grass, even though she couldn't see it! She loved to feel the feathers on a fluffy chick, the fur of an animal, the coolness of the water in the creek. She loved the fragrance of the flowers, and she could identify each one that grew near the farmhouse or in the meadow. She liked the odor of the cedar trees and the smell of firecrackers as they burst in the summer air.

Best of all she liked to listen. She could hear many faraway noises as well as those nearby. She heard the sound of the horn which a cake vendor blew as he rode his bike through the street of the nearby village, trying to sell his bean-curd cakes. She caught the sound of the temple bell which the wind carried from the faraway mountain. She liked best the sound of the gentle wind, blowing through the rice fields, saying, *"Zawa, zawa, zawa."*

Sachi used to sit or stand still, with her eyes closed tight, listening to the many kinds of sound. In the spring she was usually awakened by the sound of her mother chopping white radishes to put into the soy-bean soup which they had for breakfast almost every day the year round. The chopping said, *"Ton-ton! Ton-ton! Ton-ton-ton-ton!"*

At the same time she could hear her father washing his hoes and spades, getting ready for his work on the farm. The washing sound was, *"Goshi-goshi. Goshi-goshi."*

After breakfast the other people in Sachi's family left home. Her parents went to the farm and her brother to school. His dog followed him, saying, *"Wan-wan! Wan-wan-wan!"* Only Sachi and her old cat stayed at home.

Sachi almost always stayed in the house until nearly noon when she heard the hens cackle, *"Koke-ko-ko! Koke-ko-ko!"*

"Listen!" said Sachi to her cat. "Do you hear the hens say, 'Koke-ko-ko! Koke-ko-ko'? Are they saying, 'One egg' or 'Two eggs' today?"

The old cat loked at Sachi, but he didn't bother to answer.

Gathering eggs was Sachi's job, and it had been her job as long as she, or the cat, could remember.

Sachi went quickly to the cages, with the old cat following at her heels. She knelt down and swinging her hands back and forth over the nests, she found an egg. She held the newly laid egg close to her cheek because she liked the smooth, round, lukewarm feeling.

Then, holding the egg gently in one hand, she carefully felt all over the nests with her other hand. Back and forth, from side to side, deeper and deeper into the nests she felt, making sure that she did not miss an egg. Sure enough, at the very back of the nest, almost in the corner, lay another egg.

"Two eggs today," sang Sachi.

She turned; and holding an egg in each hand, she walked slowly back to the house, counting her steps as she went. She certainly didn't want to stumble now—not with two eggs in her hands!

Just as she reached the kitchen door, Sachi stopped, drew a long deep breath, and listened.

"This is a happy day," she said to her faithful cat who was close beside her. "I can smell the blossoms on the plum tree. I can hear the wind in the rice field. I can feel two warm eggs in my hands."

As the old cat listened, he too heard the wind gently say, *"Zawa, zawa, zawa."* Then the old cat purred, *"Goro, goro, goro."* It was a happy day.

—YOSHIKO YOKOCHI

# THE TOWN OF QUIET COVE

*(There are many noises in this story. Some are quiet sounds. How would you make these sounds? Paddleboat in a river? Cow? Horse? Cat? Grandmother's rocker? Some sounds are noisy. How would you make these sounds? Steamboat? Train? Car? Trolley car? Fire siren? Trucks going up a hill? Policeman's whistle? Drill? Airplane? How would a happy boy yell? Listen to the story. Make the right noise at the right time. Say the noises faster and faster, until at the end of the story, they sound like one big noise)*

Once upon a time, long ago, there was a pleasant little town called Quiet Cove. It stood on the banks of a wide, lazy river. If you listened on a quiet afternoon you could hear a paddleboat on the river go,_____; a cow in the field say,_____; a horse in the stable say,_____; a cat on the porch say, _____; grandmother's rocker go,_____; and once in a while a boy yell,_____!

Quiet Cove was a *very* quiet town, until one day people heard a new noise. It was a steamboat on the river. It went,_____. All the people wanted to ride on the steamboat that said, _____. Now on a quiet afternoon in Quiet Cove, you could hear a steamboat say,_____; a paddleboat say,_____; a cow in the field say,_____; a horse in the stable say, _____; a cat on the porch say,_____; great-grand-mother's rocker go,_____; and once in a while a boy yell, _____!

A long time went by, and the people of Quiet Cove heard a

new noise. It was a train. It went,_____. All the people wanted to ride on the train that said,_____. Now on a quiet afternoon in Quiet Cove, you could hear a train say, _____; a steamboat say,_____; a paddleboat say, _____; a cow say,_____; a horse say,_____; a cat say,_____; great-great-grandmother's rocker go, _____; and sometimes a boy yell,_____!

Many years went by, and the people of Quiet Cove heard a new noise. It was a car. It went,_____. People wanted to ride in the car that said,_____.

Now on a quiet afternoon in Quiet Cove you could hear a car say,_____; a steamboat say,_____; a train say, _____; a paddleboat say,_____; a cow say,_____; a horse say,_____; a cat say,_____; great-great-great-grandmother's rocker go,_____; and once in a while a boy yell,_____!

Before many years went by, many new noises came to Quiet Cove, one right after the other. A trolley car said,_____; a fire siren said,_____; trucks going up a hill said, _____; a policeman's whistle went,_____; a drill went,_____; and a plane overhead went,_____!

"Why do they call this Quiet Cove?" yelled a little boy named Larry.

"Well," said his grandma, getting close so that Larry could hear. "A long, long time ago, in the days of your great-great-great-grandmother, on a quiet afternoon you could hear the paddleboat on the river say,_____; the cows in the field say, _____; the horse in the stable say,_____; the cat on the porch say,_____; great-great-great-grandmother's rocker go,_____; and once in a while a boy yell,_____!

Larry yelled,_____! But no one in Quiet Cove heard him because the steamboats were saying,_____; the train went,_____; the cars went,_____; the trolley cars went,_____; the fire sirens went,_____; the trucks going up the hills said,_____; the policemen's whistles went,_____; the drill went,_____; and a plane overhead went,_____!

—BERNICE WELLS CARLSON

# POEMS WITH
# A REFRAIN

## POEMS WITH A REFRAIN

For the first time in this book, the child is expected to join the reader or storyteller in saying *words.* Each verse of each poem ends with a refrain, a simple line or group of words.

Often when a child catches the meter and rhythm of a poem, and likes the swing and sound of the words, he will join happily in saying one line although he is not yet ready to memorize a poem. He will listen intently until he knows it is time to say the line he wants to say. If a child does not choose to join in saying the refrain, don't force him.

These poems may be used for simplified group choral speaking. One person may say or read the verse with the group joining in the refrain.

## A LADY IN WHITE

*(Join in saying the refrain, "Puff, puff! Swish, swish! Floating on high." If you wish swing your arms as the wind lifts the lady and she floats in the sky)*

A lady in white
Combed her hair so high
A puff of wind
Blew her up in the sky.
*Puff, puff! Swish, swish!*
*Floating on high.*

Is that a cloud
Up in the sky?
No, a lady in white
Combed her hair too high.
*Puff, puff! Swish, swish!*
*Floating on high.*

—BERNICE WELLS CARLSON

## GOOD-BYE, IMPEY

*(Say the refrain together)*

Who tracked that mud upon the floor?
Who just went out and slammed the door?
*Must be Impey!*

Who left his jeans upon the chair?
Who threw waste paper over there?
*Must be Impey!*

Who came to dinner very late?
Who grabbed the cookies from the plate?
*Must be Impey!*

Who hollers back and won't say "please"?
Who is a nuisance and a tease?
*Must be Impey!*

If Impey comes around today,
Don't be surprised if we should say,
*Good-bye, Impey!*

—BERNICE WELLS CARLSON

## THE LIGHT-HEARTED FAIRY

*(At the end of each verse, join in saying the refrain, "With a hey, and a heigh, and a ho!")*

Oh, who is so merry, so merry, heigh ho!
As the light-hearted fairy? Heigh ho! Heigh ho!
   He dances and sings
   To the sound of his wings,
*With a hey, and a heigh, and a ho!*

Oh, who is so merry, so airy, heigh ho!
As the light-hearted fairy? Heigh ho! Heigh ho!
   His nectar he sips
   From the primroses' lips
*With a hey, and a heigh, and a ho!*

Oh, who is so merry, so merry, heigh ho!
As the light-hearted fairy! Heigh ho! Heigh ho!
   The night is his noon
   And the sun is his moon,
*With a hey, and a heigh, and a ho!*

—AUTHOR UNKNOWN

## AIKEN DRUM

*(At the end of each line of this verse, there is a refrain, "And his name was Aiken Drum." Say it together. Also act out the verse with your hands. Make a big circle with your arms for the moon. "Play upon a ladle" as you would play a fiddle. Point to each piece of clothing as it is mentioned.*

*A "haggis bag," mentioned near the end of the verse, is a Scotch dish of food. The cook mixes together liver, onions, oatmeal, seasoning, and sometimes other things, stuffs them into the lining of the stomach of an animal and boils the food. Britches made of haggis bags would look something like plastic bags stuffed with brown meat)*

There was a man lived in the moon,
*And his name was Aiken Drum.*
He played upon a ladle,
*And his name was Aiken Drum.*
And his hat was made of good green cheese,
*And his name was Aiken Drum.*
And his coat was made of good roast beef,
*And his name was Aiken Drum.*
And his buttons were made of penny loaves,
*And his name was Aiken Drum.*
And his waistcoat was made of crusts of pie,
*And his name was Aiken Drum.*
And his britches were made of haggis bags,
*And his name was Aiken Drum.*
There was a man lived in the moon.
*And his name was Aiken Drum.*

—NURSERY RHYME

# LONG, LONG AGO

*(Join in the last line of each verse)*

Winds through the olive trees
    Softly did blow,
'Round little Bethlehem
    Long, long ago.

Sheep on the hillside lay
    Whiter than snow;
Shepherds were watching them,
    Long, long ago.

Then from the happy sky,
    Angels bent low,
Singing their songs of joy,
    Long, long ago.

For in a manger bed,
    Cradled we know,
Christ came to Bethlehem
    Long, long ago.

—AUTHOR UNKNOWN

## THE KEEPER

*(Join in saying the last line of each verse,*
*"Among the leaves so green-o!")*

The Keeper did a shooting go,
And under his cloak he carried a bow,
All for to shoot a merry little doe.
*Among the leaves so green-o!*

The first doe he shot at, he missed.
The second doe he trimmed, he kissed.
The third doe went where nobody whist.
*Among the leaves so green-o!*

The fourth doe, she did cross the plain,
The Keeper fetched her back again.
Where she's now she may remain.
*Among the leaves so green-o!*

The fifth doe, she did cross the brook.
The Keeper fetched her back with his crook.
Where she's now, you must go and look,
*Among the leaves so green-o!*

—AUTHOR UNKNOWN

## I SAW THREE SHIPS

*(Say the refrain together, "On New Year's Day in the morning")*

I saw three ships come sailing by,
  Come sailing by, come sailing by.
I saw three ships come sailing by,
  *On New Year's Day in the morning.*

And what do you think was in them,
  Was in them, was in them?
And what do you think was in them,
  *On New Year's Day in the morning?*

Three pretty girls were in them,
  Were in them, were in them.
Three pretty girls were in them,
  *On New Year's Day in the morning.*

One could whistle and one could sing,
  And one could play the violin.
Such joy was there at my wedding,
  *On New Year's Day in the morning.*

—TRADITIONAL

## LITTLE ORPHANT ANNIE

*(Say together the refrain at the end of each verse)*

Little Orphant Annie's come to our house to stay,
An' wash the cups an' saucers up, an' brush the crumbs away,
An' shoo the chickens off the porch, an' dust the hearth, an' sweep,
An' make the fire, an' bake the bread, an' earn her board-an'-keep;
An' all us other children, when the supper things is done,
We set around the kitchen fire an' have the mostest fun
A-list'nin' to the witch-tales 'at Annie tells about,
*An' the Gobble-uns 'at gits you*
   *Ef you*
    *Don't*
      *Watch*
       *Out!*

Onc't they was a little boy wouldn't say his prayers—
An' when he went to bed at night, away upstairs,
His Mammy heerd him holler, an' his Daddy heerd him bawl,
An' when they turn't the kivvers down, he wasn't there at all!
And they seeked him in the rafter-room, an' cubby-hole, an' press,
An' seeked him up the chimbly-flue, an' ever'wheres, I guess;
But all they ever found wuz thist his pants an' roundabout'
*An' the Gobble-uns'll git you*
   *Ef you*
    *Don't*
      *Watch*
       *Out!*

An' one time a little girl 'ud allus laugh an' grin,
An' make fun of ever' one, an' all her blood-an'-kin;
And onc't when they was "company," an' ole folks wuz there,
She mocked 'em, an' shocked 'em, an' said she didn't care!
An' thist as she kicked her heels, an' turn't to run an' hide,
They wuz two great big Black Things a-standin' by her side,
An' they snatched her through the ceilin' 'fore she knowed what
   she's about!
*An' the Gobble-uns'll git you*
      *Ef you*
       *Don't*
        *Watch*
        *Out!*

An' little Orphant Annie says, when the blaze is blue,
An' the lamp-wick sputters, an' the wind goes woo-oo!
An' you hear the crickets quit, an' the moon is gray,
An' the lightnin'-bugs in dew is all squenched away,—
You better mind yer parents, and yer teachers fond an' dear,
An' churish them 'at loves you, an' dry the orphant's tear,
An' he'p the pore an' needy ones 'at clusters all about,
*'Er the Gobble-uns'll git you*
      *Ef you*
       *Don't*
        *Watch*
        *Out!*

—JAMES WHITCOMB RILEY

# WYNKEN, BLYNKEN, AND NOD

*(Say together the refrain at the end of each verse, "Wynken, Blynken, and Nod")*

Wynken, Blynken, and Nod one night
  Sailed off in a wooden shoe,—
Sailed on a river of crystal light,
  Into a sea of dew.
"Where are you going, and what do you wish?"
  The old moon asked the three.
"We have come to fish for the herring fish
  That live in this beautiful sea;
  Nets of silver and gold have we!"
    *Said Wynken,*
    *Blynken,*
    *And Nod.*

The old moon laughed and sang a song,
  As they rocked in the wooden shoe,
And the wind that sped them all night long
  Ruffled the waves of dew.
The little stars were the herring fish
  That lived in that beautiful sea—
"Now cast your nets wherever you wish—
  Never afeard are we;"
  So cried the fishermen three:
    *Wynken,*
    *Blynken,*
    *And Nod.*

All night long their nets they threw
    To the stars in the twinkling foam—
Then down from the skies came the wooden shoe,
    Bringing the fishermen home:
'Twas all so pretty a sail, it seemed
    As if it could not be.
And some folks thought 'twas a dream they dreamed
    Of sailing that beautiful sea—
    But I shall name you the fishermen three:
        *Wynken,*
        *Blynken,*
        *And Nod.*

Wynken and Blynken are two little eyes,
    And Nod is a little head,
And the wooden shoe that sailed the skies
    Is a wee one's trundle-bed.
So shut your eyes while mother sings
    Of wonderful sights that be,
And you shall see the beautiful things
    As you rock in the misty sea
    Where the old shoe rocked the fisherman three:
        *Wynken,*
        *Blynken,*
        *And Nod.*

—EUGENE FIELD

# OLD JACK FROST

*(This poem has a pattern. See how quickly you can join in saying "Old Jack Frost" at the right time)*

Who sweetens up the summer fruit?
  *Old Jack Frost!*
Who gives the tree his new fall suit?
  *Old Jack Frost!*
Who brings the walnut tumbling down?
Who makes the chestnut sweet and brown?
Who yellows up the pumpkin's gown?
  *Old Jack Frost!*

Who bites the little children's toes?
  *Old Jack Frost!*
Who causes white all out of doors?
  *Old Jack Frost!*
Who makes the rheumatism creep?
Who makes you crawl up in a heap?
And call for covers when you sleep?
  *Old Jack Frost!*

—AUTHOR UNKNOWN

## THE TALE OF JOHN HENRY PAUL BROWN

*(Join in saying, "John Henry Paul Brown" at the end of each verse)*

John Henry Paul Brown was an excellent boy,
His mother's chief treasure; his father's great joy.
He rose promptly at six, washed his face, combed his hair,
Dressed himself with dispatch, and his bed put to air.
He brought up the coal, he carried in wood—
Oh, never was a boy so re-mark-a-bly good
As Master *John Henry Paul Brown!*

When the clock struck eight-thirty, he started for school;
He never was punished; he ne'er broke a rule;
He respected his teacher, he loved each dear mate.
He never was absent; he never was late.
He doted on grammar; to spell was his joy—
Oh, never was there such a mag-nif-i-cent boy
As Master *John Henry Paul Brown!*

'Twas the night before Christmas, and John was in bed,
But he was not sleeping, for in his small head
Was the strangest idea—you never could guess
If you tried 'til next summer—and I must confess,
Though you may not believe it, I tremble with joy,
As I write of this wonderful an-gel-ic boy,
Good Master *John Henry Paul Brown.*

Santa Claus had come down the old chimney way,
And was warming his hands, when I heard someone say,
"Dear Santa, I pray you leave nothing for me;
But won't you accept these three Christmas gifts, see?
A heavier coat, a very warm hood,
And an automobile," said John Henry, the good—
Kind Master *John Henry Paul Brown.*

Old Santa gasped, and down fell his pack,
He was so surprised, kept crying, "Alack!
That I should pass hundreds of Christmases through
Before I encountered a lad just like you!
In my life I have given full many a toy,
But received not one thing, from a girl or a boy,
Save Master *John Henry Paul Brown.*"

John Henry went quietly back to his bed,
And Santa, shaking his dear old white head,
Took up John's presents and caught up his pack;
But just as I heard him again say, "Alack!"
I awoke from my dream; and I felt rather sad,
To think that there never had been such a lad—
As Master *John Henry Paul Brown!*

—INA WRIGHT HANSON

## WHO STOLE FOUR EGGS?

(*Say together the last line of each verse*)

To whit! To whit! To whee!
Will you listen to me?
Who stole four eggs I laid?
And the nice nest I made?
*To whit! To whit! To whee!*

"Not I," said the cow. "Moo-moo,
Such a thing I'd never do!
I gave you a wisp of hay
But didn't take your nest away.
*Not I," said the cow. "Moo moo.*"

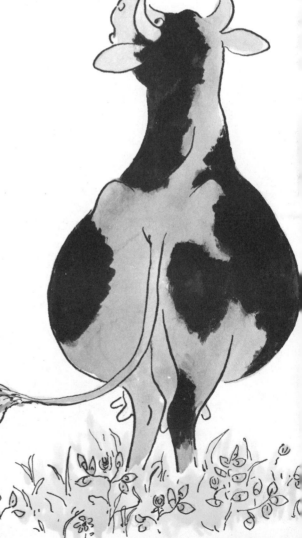

"Not I," said the dog. "Bow-wow.
I couldn't be so mean, I trow.
I gave hairs the nest to make,
But the nest I did not take.
*Not I," said the dog. "Bow-wow!"*

To whit! To whit! To whee!
Will you listen to me?
Who stole four eggs I laid?
And the nice nest I made?
*To whit! To whit! To whee!*

"Not I," said the sheep. "Baa baa.
I could not be so bad.
I gave wool the nest to line,
But the nest was not mine.
*Not I," said the sheep. "Baa baa."*

"Not I," said the hen. "Cluck, cluck.
Stealing eggs will bring bad luck.
I haven't a chick that
Would do such a trick.
*Not I," said the hen. "Cluck, cluck."*

To whit! To whit! To whee!
Will you listen to me?
Who stole four eggs I laid?
And the nice nest I made?
*To whit! To whit! To whee!*

"I did," said a boy. "I'm sorry too.
It was a mean thing to do.
As you probably guessed,
I stole the nest.
*I did," said the boy. "I'm sorry too."*

—ADAPTED FROM A POEM BY LYDIA MARIA CHILD

# POEMS WITH
# A CHORUS

## POEMS WITH A CHORUS

The story poems in this section have a simple chorus at the end of each verse. Reader and child may repeat the chorus together.

A child can learn a two-line chorus by listening to it. Do not try to drill him. Even when he likes a poem with a longer chorus he may want to join you in saying only a part of the chorus. If he is able to read he may want to read the chorus with you until he has memorized it.

These poems may be used for simple group choral speaking, with one person reading or reciting the verse and the group joining in the chorus.

## ZIPPETY, ZIPPETY, ZIM, ZIM, ZIM!

*(Before you read the poem, sing the chorus to any tune you wish; or say it in a sing-song voice. Pretend to strum a ukulele. Now read the poem and sing or say the chorus together. On the word "you" in second line of last verse, shake the hand of a person near you.)*

Miss Quimby came from Kankakee,
And great were tales she told to me
Of knights so bold and ladies fair;
Of gnomes and elves without a care.
She sang a tune quite short and gay
And always at the end she'd say,
"Who sings this song from start to end
Will ever be your special friend."
Chorus: *Zippety Zippety! Zim, zim, zim!* (*Sing briskly*)
   *Zippety, zim! Zippety, zim!*
   *Zippety! Zippety! Zim, zim, zim!*
   *Zippety! Zippety! Zoop-a-laa!*

148

I grew too old for maidens fair
And gnomes and elves without a care.
I played baseball. I rode my bike.
I liked to swim. I liked to hike.
But sometimes in the dead of night,
When all alone without a light,
I'd sing my song, from start to end,
And dream about a special friend.

> *Zippety! Zippety! Zim, zim, zim!*    (*Sing dreamily*)
> *Zippety, zim! Zippety, zim!*
> *Zippety! Zippety! Zim, zim, zim!*
> *Zippety! Zippety! Zoop-a-laa!*

I joined the Navy and traveled far
From Greenland down to Zanzibar,
From Port-au-Prince to old Hong Kong;
And then, back home, I heard my song.
I heard my song from start to end
And knew at once I'd found my friend.

> *Zippety! Zippety! Zim, zim, zim!*    (*Sing happily*)
> *Zippety, zim! Zippety, zim!*
> *Zippety! Zippety! Zim, zim, zim!*
> *Zippety! Zippety! Zoop-a-laa!*

Who sang my song from start to end?
You!                (*Shake hand of person near you*)
You sang my song from start to end.
I know you are my special friend!

> *Zippety! Zippety! Zim, zim, zim!*
> *Zippety, zim! Zippety, zim!*
> *Zippety! Zippety! Zim, zim, zim!*
> *Zippety! Zippety! Zoop-a-laa!*

—BERNICE WELLS CARLSON

## MY VERY OWN PET

*(Make the sound of each pet at the right time in the poem)*

I had a little puppy,
The nicest puppy yet;
And that little puppy
Was my very own pet.
That little puppy said, *"Bow-wow-wow!"*
*With a bow, and a wow, and a bow-wow-wow!*

I had a little kitty,
The nicest kitty yet;
And that little kitty,
Was my very own pet.
And that little kitty said, *"Meow, meow, meow!"*
And that little puppy said, *"Bow-wow-wow!"*
*With a bow, and a wow, and a bow-wow-wow!*

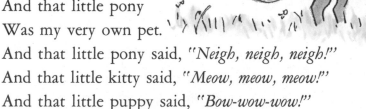

I had a little pony,
The nicest pony yet;
And that little pony
Was my very own pet.
And that little pony said, *"Neigh, neigh, neigh!"*
And that little kitty said, *"Meow, meow, meow!"*
And that little puppy said, *"Bow-wow-wow!"*
*With a bow, and a wow, and a bow-wow-wow!"*

I had a little duck,
The nicest duck yet;
And that little duck
Was my very own pet.
And that little duck said, *"Quack, quack, quack!"*
And that little pony said, *"Neigh, neigh, neigh!"*
And that little kitty said, *"Meow, meow, meow!"*
And that little puppy said, *"Bow-wow-wow!"*
*With a bow, and a wow, and a bow-wow-wow!*

(*Add as many verses as you wish. After each new verse repeat
the sounds of the animals of all the preceding verses but ending with
"With a bow, and a wow, and a bow-wow-wow"*)

And that little hen said, *"Cluck, cluck, cluck!"*
And that little bird said, *"Peep, peep, peep!"*
And that little calf said, *"Moo, moo, moo!"*
And that little sheep said, *"Baa, baa, baa!"*

—BERNICE WELLS CARLSON

## GRASSHOPPER GREEN

(*Say together the chorus at the end of each verse*)

Grasshopper Green is a comical chap;
  He lives on the best of fare.
Bright little trousers, jacket, and cap,
  These are his summer wear.
Out in the meadow he loves to go
  Playing away in the sun.
*Chorus: It's hopperty, skipperty, high and low,*
  *Summer's the time for fun.*

Grasshopper Green has a dozen wee boys;
  And as soon as their legs are strong
Each of them joins in his frolicsome joys,
  Singing his merry song.
Under the hedge they love to go
  Soon as the day's begun.
  *It's hopperty, skipperty, high and low,*
  *Summer's the time for fun.*

Grasshopper Green has a quaint little house;
  It's under the hedge so gay,
Grandmother Spider, as still as a mouse,
  Watches him over the way.
Gladly he's calling the children, I know,
  Out in the beautiful sun.
  *It's hopperty, skipperty, high and low,*
  *Summer's the time for fun.*

—AUTHOR UNKNOWN

# OUR THANKSGIVING DINNER

*(This poem has a chorus that grows. Say the chorus together)*

"I'll roast Thanksgiving turkey,"
My grandma said to me.
"It will be the biggest turkey
That ever you did see."
*Chorus: So Grandma roasted turkey,*
  *And, oh, it was so good!*
  *We all gave thanks*
  *For family, friends, and food.*

"I will make some big mince pies,"
Said Miss Ann who lives next door.
"I make such very good mince pies
Folks always ask for more."
*Chorus: So Miss Ann made mince pies.*
  *Grandma roasted turkey,*
  *And, oh, it was so good!*
  *We all gave thanks*
  *For family, friends, and food.*

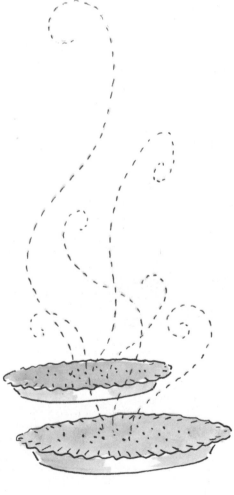

Mom said, "I will bake some squash."
Nan said, "I will peel potatoes."
Jean said, "I will mix a salad
Of greens and ripe tomatoes."
*Chorus: So Jean mixed a salad.*
  *Nan peeled potatoes.*
  *Mom baked some squash.*
  *Miss Ann made mince pies.*
  *Grandma roasted turkey,*
  *And, oh, it was so good!*
  *We all gave thanks*
  *For family, friends, and food.*

Dad said, "I'll sharpen knives
Before the meal is ready."
"And I will crack some nuts,"
Said my brother Freddie.
*Chorus: So Freddie cracked nuts.*
  *Dad sharpened knives.*
  *Jean mixed a salad.*
  *Nan peeled potatoes.*
  *Mom baked some squash.*
  *Miss Ann made mince pies.*
  *Grandma roasted turkey,*
  *And, oh, it was so good!*
  *We all gave thanks*
  *For family, friends, and food.*

154

Grandpa said, "I'll bring apples.
They were very good this fall."
I thought and thought and then I said,
"I guess I'll help you all."
*Chorus: So I helped everyone.*
   *Grandpa brought apples.*
   *Freddie cracked nuts.*
   *Dad sharpened knives.*
   *Jean mixed a salad.*
   *Nan peeled potatoes.*
   *Mom baked some squash.*
   *Miss Ann made mince pies.*
   *Grandma roasted turkey,*
   *And, oh, it was so good!*
   *We all gave thanks*
   *For family, friends, and food.*

—BERNICE WELLS CARLSON

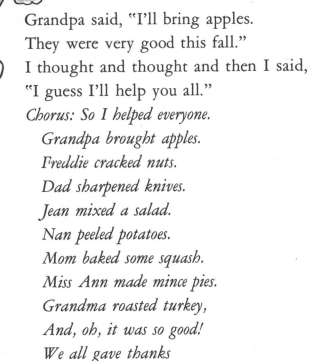

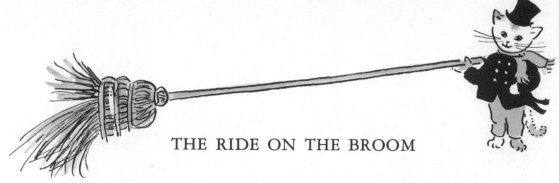

# THE RIDE ON THE BROOM

*(Learn the chorus. Say it together after every verse, changing the way you say it in accordance with the mood of each verse)*

There was an old woman who rode on a broom.
She took her Tom kitten along as a groom.
*Chorus: With a highgee, hogee, humble;*
*And a bimble, bamble, bumble!*

They traveled along 'til they came to the sky.
The kitten got hungry and started to cry.
*With a highgee, hogee, humble;*
*With a bimble, bamble, bumble!*

"We need a big thermos and lunch in a sack.
There's nothing to eat here; please let's go back."
*With a highgee, hogee, humble;*
*With a bimble, bamble, bumble!*

The woman refused to go back quite so soon.
She wanted to visit the man in the moon.
*With a highgee, hogee, humble;*
*And a bimble, bamble, bumble!*

Said Tom, "I'll go back to my very own house;
For there I can catch a good rat or a mouse."
*With a highgee, hogee, humble;*
*And a bimble, bamble, bumble!*

"But pray," said the woman, "how will you go?"
You can't have my broomstick, I'll have you know."
   *With a highgee, hogee, humble;*
   *And a bimble, bamble, bumble!*

"Never mind," said Tom, "I've a way of my own!"
He slid down a rainbow and left her alone.
   *With a highgee, hogee, humble;*
   *And a bimble, bamble, bumble!*

*Whee-eee-ee-e!*       *(Draw out this last sound for the effect*
                       *of a cat sliding down a rainbow)*

—ADAPTED FROM OLD NURSERY RHYME

157

## THE MAIDEN IN THE CASTLE

*(After each line, join in saying the chorus together. Change your tone according to the mood of the poem)*

In a castle sits a maid.
*Chorus: Ding dong! Ding, ding dong!*      *(Gaily)*
  *All among the roses.*

A knight comes riding to her aid.
  *Ding dong! Ding, ding dong!*      *(Faster)*
  *All among the roses.*

I can hear the maiden sigh.
  *Ding dong! Ding, ding dong!*      *(Slowly)*
  *All among the roses.*

A wall is there. The wall is high.
  *Ding dong! Ding, ding dong!*      *(Firmly)*
  *All among the roses.*

I will break down half the wall.
  *Ding dong! Ding, ding dong!*      *(With determination)*
  *All among the roses.*

Still more wall will have to fall.
  *Ding dong! Ding, ding dong!*      *(Louder but slower)*
  *All among the roses.*

To break it all I'm not afraid.
  *Ding dong! Ding, ding dong!*     (*Louder and firmer*)
  *All among the roses.*

Now I see the lovely maid!
  *Ding dong! Ding, ding dong!*     (*Happily*)
  *All among the roses.*

—AUTHOR UNKNOWN

## TWITTER-HOOO-OO!

(*Say the chorus together*)

The owl among the bushes sat;
And when it rained, it spoiled his hat;
But when it dried, he said, "Oh, bosh!
It's all the better for the wash."
*Chorus: Twitter-hooo-oo! Twitter-hooo-oo!*
  *We'll do as other people do.*

The owl stood on a mossy wall,
And there began to hoot and call.
The moon arose; he flapped his wing.
Said he, "She comes to hear me sing."
  *Twitter-hooo-oo! Twitter-hooo-oo!*
  *We'll do as other people do.*

—MOTHER GOOSE FROM GERMANY

159

## THE LITTLE ELF

*(Laugh, Ha, ha! Ha, ha! Ha, ha! Ha, ha! and repeat the last line of
the verse)*

I met a little elf-man once
Down where the lilies blow;
I asked him why he was so small
And why he did not grow.
   *Ha, ha! Ha, ha! Ha, ha! Ha, ha!*
   *And why he did not grow.*

He slightly frowned and with his eyes
He looked me through and through.
"I'm quite as big for me," he said,
"As you are big for you."
   *Ha, ha! Ha, ha! Ha, ha! Ha, ha!*
   *As you are big for you.*

—AUTHOR UNKNOWN

# GNOR THE GNOME

*(Say the chorus together)*

Gnor is a gnome, and he makes his home
In the oak tree, hollow and dark.
The wind of the sky brings fear to his eye,
Lest it choose his house for a mark.
*Chorus: Blow, North Wind, blow! Blow, North Wind, blow!*
*The gnome is safe in the old oak tree,*
*Away from the wind and the snow.*

And that is why, aright and awry,
The gnome twists the oak tree's roots—
To anchor his house when the leaves fly by,
The red leaves that the North Wind loots.
*Blow, North Wind, blow! Blow, North Wind, blow!*
*The gnome is safe in the old oak tree,*
*Away from the wind and the snow.*

He hides away in the tree trunk warm
While the song of the North Wind rings.
The night marches by in step with the storm
As its lantern of lightning swings.
*Blow, North Wind, blow! Blow, North Wind, blow!*
*The gnome is safe in the old oak tree,*
*Away from the wind and the snow.*

—ADAPTED BY BERNICE WELLS CARLSON FROM A POEM BY RUDOLPH BUNNER

# THE FOX AND THE GOOSE

*(Say the chorus together)*

The fox went out on a frosty night,
And begged the moon to give him a light.
He had many miles to walk that night
Before he reached his den, oh.
*Chorus: Den, oh! Den, oh!*
  *Before he reached his den, oh!*

The fox caught the gray goose by the neck
And flung her quickly across his back.
The black ducks shouted, "Quack! quack, quack!
The fox is off to his den, oh."
  *Den, oh! Den, oh!*
  *The fox is off to his den, oh!*

Mrs. Slipper Slapper jumped out of bed.
Out of the window she popped her head.
"John! John, the old gray goose is gone.
The fox is off to his den, oh."
 *Den, oh! Den, oh!*
 *The fox is off to his den, oh!*

John went up the top of the hill,
And blew a long blast both loud and shrill.
The fox said, "That's quite pretty. Still—
I'd rather be in my den, oh."
 *Den, oh! Den, oh!*
 *I'd rather be in my den, oh.*

The goose he took to his hungry wife,
Who made good use of her carving knife.
"Never ate better goose in my life.
We're happy here in our den, oh."
*Den, oh! Den, oh!*
*We're happy here in our den, oh!*

—AUTHOR UNKNOWN. *Adapted by*
*Bernice Wells Carlson from traditional verse*

## THE PEPPERY MAN

*(Join in the chorus after each verse)*

The Peppery Man was cross and thin.
He scolded out and he scolded in.
He shook his fist; his hair he tore.
He stamped his feet and slammed the door.
*Chorus: Heigh, ho, the Peppery Man!*
  *The rabid, crabbed, Peppery Man!*
  *Oh, never since the world began*
  *Was anyone like the Peppery Man!*

His ugly temper was so sour,
He often scolded for an hour.
He gnashed his teeth and stormed and scowled.
He snapped and snarled and yelled and howled.
  *Heigh, ho, the Peppery Man!*
  *The rabid, crabbed, Peppery Man!*
  *Oh, never since the world began*
  *Was anyone like the Peppery Man!*

He wore a fierce and savage frown.
He scolded up and he scolded down.
He scolded over field and glen.
Then he scolded back again.
  *Heigh, ho, the Peppery Man!*
  *The rabid, crabbed Peppery Man!*
  *Oh, never since the world began,*
  *Was anyone like the Peppery Man!*

His neighbors when they heard his roars,
Closed the blinds and locked their doors;
Shut their windows, sought their beds,
Stopped their ears and covered their heads.
  *Heigh, ho, the Peppery Man!*
  *The rabid, crabbed Peppery Man!*
  *Never since the world began,*
  *Was anyone like the Peppery Man!*

He fretted, chafed, and boiled, and fumed.
With fiery rage he was consumed;
And no one knew when he was vexed,
What in the world would happen next.
  *Heigh, ho, the Peppery Man!*
  *The rabid, crabbed, Peppery Man!*
  *Never since the world began,*
  *Was anyone like the Peppery Man!*

—ARTHUR MACY

## THE COOKY-NUT TREE

(*Say the last line of the witch's chant together. If you would like to learn the entire chant, say it at the right time*)

Oh, the Pilliwinks lived by the portals of Loo,
    In the land of the Pullicum-wees,
Where gingerbread soldiers and elephants grew
    On the top of the cooky-nut trees.
And the Pilliwinks gazed at them, wondering how
    They could get at those goodies so brown;
And the ginger-men danced on the cooky-nut bough,
    And the elephants wouldn't come down.

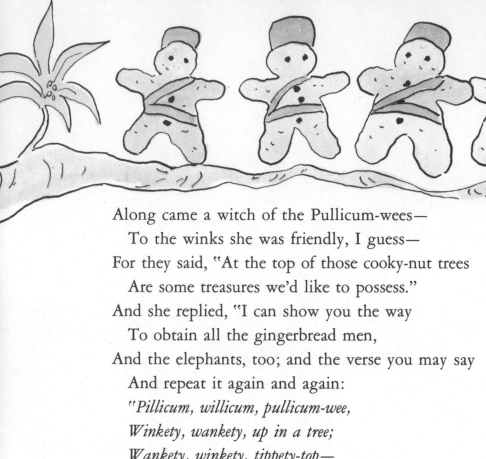

Along came a witch of the Pullicum-wees—
   To the winks she was friendly, I guess—
For they said, "At the top of those cooky-nut trees
   Are some treasures we'd like to possess."
And she replied, "I can show you the way
   To obtain all the gingerbread men,
And the elephants, too; and the verse you may say
   And repeat it again and again:
   *"Pillicum, willicum, pullicum-wee,*
   *Winkety, wankety, up in a tree;*
   *Wankety, winkety, tippety-top—*
   Down *come the cooky-nuts, hippety-hop!"*

Then all the Pilliwinks stood in a row,
   And repeated the magical song,
Till elephants eagerly hastened below,
   And soldiers marched down in a throng.
And for many long years, by the portals of Loo,
   The Pilliwink people you'd see
Enticing the gingerbread goodies that grew
   At the top of the cooky-nut tree.
   *"Pillicum, willicum, pullicum-wee,*
   *Winkety, wankety, up in a tree;*
   *Wankety, winkety, tippety-top—*
   Down *come the cooky-nuts, hippety-hop!"*

—ALBERT BIGLOW PAINE

# A FROG HE WOULD A-WOOING GO

*(Say the refrain and chorus together)*

A frog he would a-wooing go.
  *"Heigho," says Rowley.*
Whether his mother would let him or no;
  *With a rowley, powley, gammon, and spinach.*
  *"Heigho," says Rowley.*

So he sat off with his opera hat.
  *"Heigho," says Rowley.*
And on the road he met a rat.
  *With a rowley, powley, gammon, and spinach.*
  *"Heigho," says Rowley.*

"Pray, Mr. Rat, will you go with me?"
  *"Heigho," says Rowley.*
"Kind Mrs. Mouse for to see."
  *With a rowley, powley, gammon, and spinach.*
  *"Heigho," says Rowley.*

When they came to the door of Mousey's hall,
  *"Heigho," says Rowley.*
They gave a loud tap, and they gave a loud call.
  *With a rowley, powley, gammon, and spinach.*
  *"Heigho," says Rowley.*

"Pray, Mrs. Mouse, are you within?"
  *"Heigho," says Rowley.*

"Yes, kind sirs, sitting and spin."
  *With a rowley, powley, gammon, and spinach.*
  *"Heigho," says Rowley.*

"Pray, Mr. Frog, will you give us a song?"
  *"Heigho," says Rowley.*
"But let it be something that's not too long."
  *With a rowley, powley, gammon, and spinach.*
  *"Heigho," says Rowley.*

"Indeed, Mrs. Mouse," replied the frog,
  *"Heigho," says Rowley.*
"A cold has made me hoarse as a frog."
  *With a rowley, powley, gammon, and spinach.*
  *"Heigho," says Rowley.*

"Since you caught a cold," Mrs. Mousey said,
  *"Heigho," says Rowley.*
"I'll sing a song that I have just made."
  *With a rowley, powley, gammon, and spinach.*
  *"Heigho," says Rowley.*

But while they were a merrymaking,
  *"Heigho," says Rowley.*
A cat and her kittens came tumbling in.
  *With a rowley, powley, gammon, and spinach.*
  *"Heigho," says Rowley.*

The cat seized the Rat by the crown.
  *"Heigho," says Rowley.*
The kitten pulled the little Mouse down.
  *With a rowley, powley, gammon, and spinach.*
  *"Heigho," says Rowley.*

This put the Frog in a terrible fright.
  *"Heigho," says Rowley.*
He took his hat and wished them goodnight.
  *With a rowley, powley, gammon, and spinach.*
  *"Heigho," says Rowley.*

As Froggy was crossing over a brook,
  *"Heigho," says Rowley.*
A little white duck came and gobbled him up.
  *With a rowley, powley, gammon, and spinach.*
  *"Heigho," says Rowley.*

So here is the end of one, two, three.
  *"Heigho," says Rowley.*
The rat, the mouse, and the little froggy.
  *With a rowley, powley, gammon, and spinach.*
  *"Heigho," says Rowley.*

—TRADITIONAL

# INDEX